A PRIEST ANSWERS 27 QUESTIONS YOU NEVER THOUGHT TO ASK

A PRIEST ANSWERS

27 QUESTIONS

You *NEVER* THOUGHT TO ASK

Father Michael Kerper

SOPHIA INSTITUTE PRESS
Manchester, New Hampshire

Copyright © 2016 by Father Michael Kerper

The questions and answers reproduced in this book were originally published in *Parable*, the magazine of the Diocese of Manchester. Bishop Peter Libasci and the *Parable* staff are grateful to Father Kerper for sharing his knowledge of our Church as well as his wit and wisdom. For more information about *Parable* or to read all of Father Kerper's articles, visit www.catholicnh.org.

All rights reserved.

Cover and interior design by Perceptions Design Studio.

No part of this book may be reproduced, stored in a retrieval system, or transmitted in any form, or by any means, electronic, mechanical, photocopying, or otherwise, without the prior written permission of the publisher, except by a reviewer, who may quote brief passages in a review.

Biblical references in this book are taken from the Catholic Edition of the Revised Standard Version of the Bible, copyright 1965, 1966 by the Division of Christian Education of the National Council of the Churches of Christ in the United States of America. Used by permission. All rights reserved.

Excerpts from the *Catechism of the Catholic Church*, Second Edition, for use in the United States of America, copyright © 1994 and 1997, United States Catholic Conference—Libreria Editrice Vaticana. Used by permission. All rights reserved.

Quotes from English translations of papal encyclicals are from the Vatican website (w2.vatican.va) © Libreria Editrice Vaticana. All rights reserved. Used with permission.

Sophia Institute Press
Box 5284, Manchester, NH 03108
1-800-888-9344
www.SophiaInstitute.com

Sophia Institute Press® is a registered trademark of Sophia Institute.

Library of Congress Cataloging-in-Publication Data

Names: Kerper, Michael (Priest), author.
Title: A priest answers 27 questions you never thought to ask / Father
    Michael Kerper.
Other titles: Priest answers twenty-seven questions you never thought to ask
Description: Manchester, New Hampshire : Sophia Institute Press, 2017. |
    Includes bibliographical references.
Identifiers: LCCN 2016054529 | ISBN 9781622829514 (pbk. : alk. paper)
Subjects: LCSH: Catholic Church—Doctrines.
Classification: LCC BX1751.3 .K468 2017 | DDC 230/.2—dc23 LC record available at
    https://lccn.loc.gov/2016054529

CONTENTS

Acknowledgments 1

PART I
Fear, Trembling, and Sweaty Hands: Our Life in the Church

1. Did Jesus actually give us the Lord's Prayer?. 5
2. Can the divorced receive Communion? 9
3. Why did I have to wait to be confirmed? 13
4. Holding hands and kissing: Why does everyone do something different at Mass? 17
5. What's the difference between mortal and venial sins? . . 23
6. What is and isn't a heresy? 27
7. How should we fast? 31
8. Are we required to give to everyone who asks for something? 35
9. What is the Act of Contrition? Why is it so important? . . 39

PART II

The New Evangelization and Old Neighbors: Our Life in the World

10. What is God's name? 45
11. Why can't women be priests? 51
12. Why doesn't Pope Francis like pets? 57
13. Can a non-Catholic be a godparent for my child? 61
14. Why can't we have a Catholic wedding at our favorite inn? 65
15. How do I explain about receiving Communion to my non-Catholic relatives? 69

PART III

Baptize, Marry, and Bury: Our Life in the World to Come

16. Who can receive Last Rites? 75
17. Can Catholics believe in reincarnation? 79
18. Is damnation real? 83
19. Whatever happened to Limbo? 87
20. Is it okay to be cremated? 91
21. Do ghosts really exist? 95

22. What is a plenary indulgence?. 99

23. Can every sin, even abortion, be forgiven? 105

PART IV
Our Peculiar Ecumenical Family: Our Faith and the Odd Traditions

24. Why are the psalms so violent?. 113

25. Was Christ born on Christmas? And what does Santa have to do with it? 117

26. Why do priests get moved? Why do deacons do so much of the priestly work now?. 123

27. Are Guardian Angels real?. 131

About the Author: Father Michael Kerper 135

Acknowledgments

We learn to answer questions well by observing the techniques of good, truthful, prudent, well-informed people. Throughout my life God has blessed me by bringing me into contact with many people worthy of imitation.

Whenever I succeed in giving a satisfying answer to someone, I always remember the two sources of any success I may have enjoyed: the Sisters, Servants of the Immaculate Heart of Mary, who taught me in grade school; and Dr. Germain Grisez, my professor of moral theology at Mount St. Mary's Seminary.

The Sisters, reknowned for teaching English, stressed order, clarity, and precision in writing and speaking. We learned that language makes us "God-like." Hence it should always be used to propose truth in a convincing and attractive way.

From Dr. Grisez, I learned the importance of respecting those who ask the questions, understanding clearly what's being asked, knowing the fullness of Catholic tradition, and responding with compassion, charity, and balance. Dr. Grisez's works, frequently presented as answers to questions, have always impressed me as excellent models to follow.

The Sisters and Dr. Grisez did much more than merely demonstrate technique. They "lived" their answers, putting into practice what they taught so clearly. Whatever may be useful in this little book flows from their rigor in teaching, their wisdom, and—most of all—their witness to the Lord's abiding truth. Thank you.

PART I

Fear, Trembling, and Sweaty Hands: Our Life in the Church

·· 1 ··
Did Jesus actually give us the Lord's Prayer?

Dear Father Kerper,

I have three questions about the Lord's Prayer. First, can we be sure that Jesus actually wrote it? I've read somewhere that the Church made it up after He died. Second, isn't it very misleading to call God "Father" all the time? God is bigger than any single image, and "Father" seems too narrow. Third, why does the version used at Mass keep very old-fashioned words such as "thy" and "hallowed"? They seem so out of place.

Thank you for your questions. Because almost every Christian knows the Our Father by heart and because we say it so frequently, we may eventually find it stale, boring, and even obsolete. And so probing questions like yours, which force us to take a critical look at the Our Father, can deepen our understanding of this simple yet glorious prayer.

Jesus as the source

Some people instantly dismiss Jesus as the real author of the Our Father because the New Testament contains two versions: the long one in Saint Matthew (6:9-13) and the short one in Saint Luke (11:2-4). Pope Benedict XVI frankly admitted this in his beautiful book *Jesus of Nazareth*. He made this crucial comment: "The discussion of which text is more original is not superfluous, but neither is it the main issue. In both versions we are praying with Jesus."[1]

Here, as always, we must remember that when Jesus preached, He never had stenographers on hand to write down every word precisely. Rather, His disciples listened to Him very carefully and soon repeated His words to others. Constant repetition over time produced a collection of very reliable memories of His shorter sayings and longer statements, such as the Our Father, which is the only prayer He left to us intact. Eventually, the Gospel writers transformed these "oral traditions" into texts, which are very reliable, although certainly not as precise as a court reporter's transcript today.

In defense of the Lord's "authorship" of the Our Father, I cite John P. Meier, a highly rigorous, careful, and immensely knowledgeable Scripture scholar. In volume 4 of his massive work *A Marginal Jew: Rethinking the Historical Jesus*, Father Meier stated that there is "a fairly secure judgment that some primitive form of the Lord's Prayer goes back to Jesus."[2]

---

[1] Pope Benedict XVI, *Jesus of Nazareth* (San Francisco: Ignatius Press, 2008), 133.

[2] John P. Meier, *A Marginal Jew: Rethinking the Historical Jesus* (New Haven: Yale University Press, 2009), 71.

In light of this scholarly assessment, we can safely reaffirm what Pope Benedict said so succinctly and beautifully: "We are praying with Jesus." Think of what happens: whenever we say the Our Father, we have within our mouths and minds the essential prayer uttered by the Lord. For this reason the priest at Mass always introduces the Lord's Prayer by saying, "We dare to say." With wonder and awe we allow the Son's prayer to flow through us to the Father.

God as Father

I fully agree with you that "Father" is a "narrow" image of God. After all, God is neither male nor female, has no physical dimensions, and can never be adequately portrayed.

However, the Our Father's most marvelous element is precisely the Lord's command to address God as Father—not Creator, not Lord, not Friend, not even "God." Here, unfortunately, we run into a problem with translation. Jesus spoke Aramaic. With just one exception, he always addressed God as "Abba," the term used by children when speaking to their fathers. In English, the equivalent word would be "Daddy" or some other informal term. The Greek text uses the word "Pater," which our translation renders as "Father." The problem, of course, is that our familiar translation cannot convey the astounding and very touching intimacy that exists between the Father/Abba and the Son.

To remedy this linguistic deficiency, we must always strive to hear the "Abba/Daddy" underneath "Father/Pater." This is crucial, for only then can we realize the "miracle" of the Our Father: Jesus has graciously permitted us to speak to His Father in exactly the same way He does.

Moreover, this is not about mere words. Rather, the privilege of praying the Our Father powerfully reminds us of an essential truth: we are indeed the adopted sons and daughters of God who enter into a deeply intimate relationship with the Father of Jesus, who joins Himself to us. The "our" of the Our Father signifies our union with the Son, not just with our fellow believers.

As to calling God "Our Mother," we must remember that when we pray the Lord's Prayer, we must become fully united with Christ. As such, we must enter into His actual experience as it truly is. This includes His "parentage" — Jesus has one true father, who is God, and a one true mother, who is Mary. We have the same "spiritual parentage." By replacing "Father" with "Mother," "Creator," or some other gender-free term, we distort the intimate relationship between Father and Son, which we share, and revert to something much inferior to what the Lord offers.

Old-fashioned language

Although Mass text translations tend to change over time, the Our Father has been left untouched for many years. Strange words such as "hallowed" for "make holy" and "trespasses" for "sins" have been left alone for the sake of stable familiarity, which makes it possible for Catholics and other Christians to pray the one prayer that comes from the Lord's own mouth. And so, we continue to "dare to say ... 'Our Father.'"

·· 2 ··

Can the divorced receive Communion?

Dear Father Kerper,
Three years ago my husband and I divorced. Since then, I have worked hard as a single mother to raise my two children as Catholics. I have found a welcoming parish and enjoy bringing them to Mass. Recently a prominent woman who goes to that church stopped me after Mass and, in front of my children, told me that I cannot receive Communion because I'm divorced. She said I was sinning by doing so. I was devastated. Is she correct? What should I do?

You have acted wisely in seeking clarification about the woman's comment concerning divorce and Communion. At times, some Catholics, even those with much experience and devotion, pass on wrong or incomplete information. Such people usually act sincerely, so I trust you will forgive her moment of insensitivity.

Your question touches on three interrelated matters: the status of divorced Catholics who have not remarried; the connection between Communion and reconciliation; and annulments.

To begin with, divorced single Catholics, such as you, are not banned from Holy Communion. They never have been.

Three of the four Gospels, however, contain nearly identical, clear statements by Jesus prohibiting divorce. The best known text is Matthew 19:6. Jesus says: "So they are no longer two but one. What therefore God has joined together, let not man put asunder." Parallels appear in Mark 10:1-12 and Luke 16:18.

Although the Lord's opposition to divorce is indisputable, the Church has long recognized that some relationships break down, making common life impossible or even dangerous. In such cases, a sincere Catholic, after prayerful reflection and competent counsel, may seek a legal separation that perhaps culminates in a civil divorce.

Divorce, in itself, does not destroy a person's relationship with God and the Catholic Church. Indeed, over the years, I have come to know many exemplary Catholics who have endured the pain of divorce and have generously used their talents—and even their divorce experience—in the service of their fellow Christians.

Now, let's consider reconciliation before Communion. Although divorce itself is not automatically a sin, the conflict that caused the divorce may include a variety of sins such as unrelenting anger, selfishness, hypercriticism, and adultery. Surely, these require repentance. Moreover, the adamant refusal of reconciliation, not divorce itself, may require a person to abstain from Communion. I hasten to add that this advice applies to everyone, not just divorced people.

The relevant Gospel text is quite clear, at least as unvarnished as the Lord's words about divorce. In Saint Matthew's version of the Sermon on the Mount, Jesus says: "So if you are offering your gift at the altar, and there remember that your brother has something against you, leave your gift there before the altar and go; first be reconciled to your brother, and then come and offer your gift" (Matt. 5:23-24).

Jesus here makes a remarkable demand: reconciliation with one's neighbor must always precede public worship of God. And all people, not just the divorced, are held to this radical standard.

Reconciliation, of course, does not mean that divorced people must reunite and remarry. Rather, it requires forgiveness, openness, and even love of the other person—not romantic love but sober Christian love that always wills the good of the adversary, even the most obnoxious and repulsive. This may take years to accomplish.

Because of the Lord's infinite patience and understanding, I trust that He accepts even the smallest sincere impulse toward reconciliation as sufficient fulfillment of His requirement that we reconcile before worshipping. However, someone who deliberately refuses forgiveness and deepens the wounds of a ruptured relationship—marital or otherwise—should think twice before receiving Communion.

Now, let's take a quick look at annulments, a complicated matter susceptible to much misinformation.

If a divorced Catholic remarries without receiving an annulment of the previous marriage, that Catholic is prevented from receiving the sacraments of the Church. If a divorced Catholic hopes to marry within the Church, he or she will need a decree of nullity. Such a decree does not dissolve a marriage, nor does it mean that the marriage never existed. Instead, the decree simply states that the marriage was not a sacramental one and therefore not an obstacle to a subsequent marriage within the Church.

Out of respect for the sacrament of Matrimony, Church law presumes that all marriages, including those contracted by baptized people beyond the confines of the Catholic Church, are true sacramental marriages until conclusive evidence establishes the contrary.

·· 3 ··
Why did I have to wait to be confirmed?

Dear Father Kerper,
Last year at the Easter Vigil I saw a priest baptize and confirm three children who looked to be eight or nine years old. This troubled me for two reasons. First, I thought only bishops could confirm people. And second, I was sixteen when I was confirmed and had to go to classes, do service projects, and go to retreats. Why are these very young children now being confirmed without much instruction and by their parish priest?

For many Catholics of our time, what you saw happen at the Easter Vigil seems wild and new. Actually, it's traditional and old. Here's why.

In 1910, Pope Saint Pius X lowered the age of First Communion to the "age of reason" or the "age of discretion"—when a child can understand the difference between right and wrong and that bread and wine can become the Body and Blood of Christ without changing their appearances. Such understanding usually becomes possible at age seven.

At the time of the Holy Father's radical change, the age of Confirmation was also the "age of reason"—seven years old. Suddenly those entrusted with preparing children for the sacraments were faced with the difficult task of teaching them about two sacraments at once: Confirmation and Holy Eucharist. In response to the Holy Father's very fervent desire that young children receive Holy Communion, preparation for First Communion soon took precedence over Confirmation, which was then delayed for several years.

Until 1910, most people received Confirmation before First Communion, usually around age seven. Hence, the very young age is more "traditional" than the older.

Now, we must acknowledge a very peculiar situation: canon law clearly states that the normal age for First Communion and Confirmation is the "age of discretion," usually seven. In practice, however, the age of Confirmation varies from seven to eighteen, and today many people get confirmed as adults.

Why this vast age difference?

Because bishops and theologians have had very different understandings about the meaning of Confirmation, especially since the Protestant Reformation and into our own time.

Some stress the ancient belief that Confirmation, which was originally celebrated with Baptism, "seals" or "completes" a person's initiation into the Church. Confirmation, then, does not require prior instruction or a reaffirmation of Christian faith. After all, Confirmation is the gift of the Holy Spirit, not a diploma. We see this understanding at work in two Catholic practices: first, the long-standing custom among Eastern-Rite Catholics of administering Baptism, Confirmation, and Holy Eucharist together to young children, including infants; and second, the requirement that young children, even babies, be confirmed if they are in serious danger of death.

Why did I have to wait to be confirmed?

By contrast, other bishops and theologians see Confirmation primarily as the sacrament that bestows grace on the baptized faithful so as to strengthen and deepen their faith. This necessarily requires intense catechesis so that a more mature child or adult can reaffirm commitments made on his or her behalf at Baptism.

This second approach, although still predominant in many places, is actually an innovation within the tradition and is now being reconsidered.

At the moment, each bishop in the United States has authority to set the age of Confirmation in his diocese within the range of seven to eighteen. This broad flexibility recognizes the diversity of the Catholic Church and the need to adapt to differing situations of children and young people.

As to the priest administering Confirmation, this is not new. While the bishop is called the "original minister" of Confirmation, he may delegate the task of confirming to any priest. When a priest baptizes a person over seven, he is ordinarily required to confirm as well. Likewise, when a priest receives a non-Catholic baptized person into the full communion of the Catholic Church, he may confirm the new Catholic as well.

4

Holding hands and kissing: Why does everyone do something different at Mass?

Dear Father Kerper,
I attend Mass at several parishes in New Hampshire, and I'm becoming confused. In some parishes, people hold hands during the Our Father. In others, I see people raising their hands like the priest at the altar. Also, I find the sign of peace a huge distraction. Isn't it a throwback to the 1960s? More and more, I find it difficult to pray because everyone does things in a different way.

These are great questions to consider as we think about the meaning behind the words we speak and the gestures we use during Mass. Your multiple questions touch upon three interconnected issues: the importance of physical gestures in public worship; the tension between tradition and innovation; and the need to balance communal and individual preferences.

First, let's consider the role of the body in worship, something we often overlook. Human beings are a union of matter and spirit, body and soul. As such, during public worship our bodies inevitably become involved in what is primarily a spiritual activity.

Designated bodily postures correspond with specific spiritual activities. For example, we sit to listen to God's Word, we stand together when we profess the Creed, and we kneel during the times of intense awareness of the Lord's presence, notably during the Eucharistic Prayer and before and after receiving Holy Communion.

In addition to these common postures, the liturgy also has two kinds of gestures: those of the ordained leaders and those of the people. Gestures used only by the ordained include the outstretched hands when he leads prayer and offers the greetings, the movements during the Eucharistic prayer, and the act of blessing. The principal gestures of the people are the sign of peace, folded hands during prayer, and genuflection to honor and acknowledge the Eucharistic Presence.

These postures and gestures have deep meaning and should never become mere habits. Rather, they should always reflect what's happening to us spiritually.

The sign of peace

Now, let's look at tradition and change. You mentioned that you don't like the sign of peace because it's "something from the 1960s." Actually, this liturgical gesture is very ancient and packed with symbolic meaning.

Although no one can pinpoint the exact origin of the "kiss of peace," it surely existed in the early fifth century. We know this because in AD 416, Pope Innocent I corrected the bishop of

Gibbia, who insisted that the kiss of peace should be exchanged among the people before the Eucharistic Prayer. Pope Innocent I, however, insisted that the kiss of peace be exchanged after the Eucharistic Prayer and immediately before the distribution of Holy Communion. Why? To stress the necessary connection between reconciliation and worthy reception of the Eucharist. By the sixth century, the two acts had become so intertwined that those unable to receive Holy Communion because of grave sin were instructed to refrain from sharing the sign of peace.

The sign of peace still seems "new" to many people because it gradually disappeared centuries ago. It survived as a formalized gesture exchanged only among the clergy—never the people—during High Masses.

In the late 1960s, after Vatican II, the Church restored the sign of peace. Whether one likes it or not, it is definitely not an innovation but part of our genuine liturgical tradition. Moreover, recognizing that it may not work well in all conditions and cultures, the Church never mandated it but made it optional.

Holding hands

Whereas the sign of peace is a true traditional practice, the custom of holding hands during the Our Father is not. Some good people promoted this practice as a way of symbolizing and even fostering community.

It has two drawbacks. First, it draws people away from the Father, whom we address in union with Christ, by focusing too much attention on the specific community linked by hands. Second, in most places, it actually divides the worshippers because some cannot reach the hands of another person. For example, I have seen some congregations broken into six or seven groups with some people actually turned from the altar as they seek someone's hand.

What began as a sincere attempt to foster community often does the opposite: those who hold hands appear to be the "insiders" while the ones unable or unwilling to clasp someone's hand look like "outsiders."

The *orans* position

As to the custom of some people who adopt the *orans* position—the outstretched arms and hands—this too can lead to confusion. The rubrics, the official instructions to the priest, direct him to adopt that position in his role as leader. By using the bodily gesture of extended arms and hands, the priest also symbolizes the essential unity of the prayer.

Here the priest acts like the conductor of an orchestra, who alone holds the baton. Imagine what would happen if other musicians rose from their seats and wielded a baton. Confusion would reign.

Although the orans position is not prohibited, its use by people in the congregation certainly seems inappropriate and distracting. In private prayer or, say, in devotional prayer groups with a more charismatic style, the orans position might be good and useful, but not during Mass.

The need for balance

This brings us to the third point: the need for balance between the communal and personal in the liturgy. By its very nature, liturgy organizes and expresses the worship of multiple people who act as a united body. Unified worship, then, needs predictable,

Why does everyone do something different at Mass?

harmonious, understandable actions. As such, conspicuously peculiar actions, such as raising one's hands during the Our Father, become distractions that erode unity. Likewise, the adamant refusal to join in common action is equally distracting, even disruptive. I know people, for example, who adamantly refuse to give and receive the sign of peace on the grounds that it's a "new custom."

Allow me to distill all these words into one "golden rule" that flows from the demands of charity: during public worship, never do anything that draws attention to yourself or distracts other people. For sure, we all have our own likes and dislikes about the liturgy, but unity in glorifying God should always takes precedence over one's own "spiritual style" and preferences.

·· 5 ··

What's the difference between mortal and venial sins?

Dear Father Kerper,
I was told years ago that there are two kinds of sins, mortal and venial. I don't understand how a loving God could impose eternal death on a person for committing a so-called mortal sin. How can we reconcile God's mercy with a spiritual death penalty? If these sins are so deadly, why can't I find a list? And what exactly is the difference between mortal and venial sins?

Thanks for your question, which shows that you have grasped the core teaching of Christ's Gospel: that God loves us, forgives all sin, and passionately desires that all people be saved. Moreover, you are right on target when you wonder how "a spiritual death penalty" can come from God, who is infinite love.

To begin with, we have to understand that God does not impose the "mortal" penalty as a vengeful punishment for a specific sin. Rather, a grave sin generates its own lethal consequences. As such, the "death penalty" does not come from God but from the sin itself.

Let's think about traffic signs. You've probably seen those big signs on highway entrances that scream: "Wrong Way. Do Not Enter." If you ignore the warning, drive down the wrong ramp at fifty miles per hour, and collide head-on with a sixteen-wheeler, you will likely experience a "mortal penalty." To complain that the civil authority, which erected the sign, cruelly and unfairly executed you for simply violating a rule would be silly. After all, the death resulted from the head-on collision, which in turn happened because you made a free and conscious decision to ignore the sign.

To put it another way, the designation of that act—driving the wrong way on the ramp—as illegal is not what kills the violator. Rather, the act was made illegal precisely because it is always potentially deadly.

Catholic tradition identifies some specific sinful acts as "mortal" because they "kill" a person's life-giving relationship with God. Note well: God does not withdraw from the relationship with the sinner; instead, the sinner freely and knowingly pulls away from God by choosing the sin. In a sense, the sinner commits spiritual suicide. God is no vindictive executioner.

As to a list of definite mortal sins, no such list exists because no specific sinful act is automatically mortal. Three conditions must always be met. First, the act must be seriously wrong, such as a grave violation of God's moral law, especially as expressed in the Ten Commandments. Second, the sinner must know that the deed is wrong. Third, the sinner must freely consent to the act. If any condition is absent, the act, even though gravely wrong in itself, is not a true mortal sin.

Gravely wrong acts include intentionally killing the innocent, lying under oath, worshipping idols, adultery, assisted suicide,

What's the difference between mortal and venial sins?

abandoning needy parents, destroying a person's reputation, desecrating the Eucharist, and blasphemy against the Holy Spirit, which means obstinately refusing God's forgiveness. Each of these acts radically contradicts Divine Love and necessarily turns the sinner away from God, the source and sustainer of life.

Now, let's consider venial sins. "Venial" comes from the Latin word *venia*, which means "pardon," "forgiveness," or "remission of debt." These sins, though surely bad, do not "kill" the sinner because they do not turn a person completely away from God.

Some venial sins might be called "defective mortal sins," namely, gravely sinful acts committed without proper knowledge or consent. For example, a youngster who removes the Eucharist from his mouth and drops it on the floor because he fears germs or choking commits an objective act of desecration, but his lack of understanding and genuine fear prevent this from being a true mortal sin. If an adult, however, commits the same act with full knowledge and the intention of showing contempt for the Lord in the Blessed Sacrament, the moral quality of that person's act differs significantly. Surely, it should be treated as a mortal sin.

Other venial sins are slight, careless, or habitual failings and violations of God's moral law, such as lies of convenience or exaggeration, frivolous gossip, mild laziness, petty theft, and casual irreverence in church.

Thinking again about traffic regulations will help here. Venial sins are akin to going seventy-six miles per hour where the speed limit is sixty-five or parking illegally for ten minutes. Both actions violate the law and are wrong, but neither is as mortally dangerous as ignoring the "Wrong Way. Do Not Enter" sign on the highway ramp.

Although the distinction between mortal and venial sins, which comes from Scripture and the tradition of the Church, is certainly helpful, we should never use it to discover what we can get away with. Such an approach misses the point. As creatures made in the image and likeness of God and empowered by God's abundant grace to lead good and holy lives, we should always avoid every act—whether large or small—that prevents us from being what God intends us to be. We never find true happiness in sin, but only in goodness.

·· 6 ··
What is and isn't a heresy?

Dear Father Kerper,
In a Bible study group I attend, some people state that certain writers and scholars are "heretical" and others are "orthodox." These scholars are all Catholics, as far as I know. What exactly do these terms mean? How do I know for sure whether someone is heretical or orthodox?

When Catholics talk among themselves, especially about controversial religious matters, they would be wise always to use language correctly. The words "heresy" and "orthodoxy" should be used sparingly, if at all.

"Heresy" comes from the Greek word for "choice," specifically the choice to remove one or more beliefs from a complete set of interrelated propositions. Heresy, then, is not just about religion; it also exists within other fields of thought.

The Catholic Church has a very precise definition of heresy. It appears in the *Code of Canon Law*: "Heresy is the obstinate denial or obstinate doubt after the reception of baptism of some truth which is to be believed by divine and Catholic faith" (can. 751).

This definition has three key elements.

First, heresy is strictly limited to truths that are settled and indispensable teachings of the Catholic Faith. For example, it is heretical to deny the bodily Resurrection of Christ, the existence of original sin, and the divinity of Christ. The Church has always taught these truths clearly and definitively.

To insist, as some do, that the Eucharist must always be received by everyone under the forms of both bread and wine, that baptism must be done by full immersion, or that the Church should not grant annulments is not heretical. For sure, such propositions contradict established Church positions, but they do not rise to the level of heresy because they do not touch the core of Catholic Faith.

Second, because heresy is a choice against some specific belief within the complete "set" of Catholic teachings, one must first accept the "set." Hence, one must be a baptized person in full communion with the Catholic Church. In other words, only a Catholic can be a heretic. Other people may hold positions that are heretical, but they're not heretics because they never accepted the whole "set" anyway.

Third, and most important, heresy requires full knowledge, understanding, and deliberation.

This brings us to a crucial distinction found within classical Catholic theology: the difference between *formal* and *material* heresy.

In the case of formal heresy, the person must know and properly understand what the Church actually teaches and then freely reject it. This happens rarely. More often than not, someone will insist that the Church has no authority to teach about a specific matter—say, the ordination of women—or that the teaching is not really definitive.

As to material heresy, this happens every day, even among the most devout. Here a person misunderstands or misstates a key Catholic teaching, thereby unknowingly advancing a serious theological

What is and isn't a heresy?

error. This happens when a person has a partial, distorted, or unbalanced understanding of the Faith.

Now, let's consider your great question about how Catholics can know what is heretical.

The Church has a juridical process that examines accusations about heresy. After a thorough study of a person's public statements and extended dialogue to discover what the person has really said and what he really means and believes, the Church will finally declare that a person has committed heresy—or has not. Until the Church has made that judgment, no Catholic should ever accuse another of heresy. When a Catholic does so, he inadvertently does injury to our Catholic communion by inciting emotions rather than making a reasoned and justified statement.

On the positive side, the Church has the longstanding practice of providing an imprimatur for books and other publications. This Latin word simply means, "let it be printed" and indicates that the local bishop believes that the book contains nothing heretical.

Today, the imprimatur appears on most books and materials used for religious education. It also appears on some Bibles, not for the biblical content but for the footnotes, introductions, and so on.

Whereas in the past, just about every Catholic book—even some poetry!—had an imprimatur, today most do not. The lack of an imprimatur does not mean that a book is heretical.

Now that we know something about heresy, we have to consider its opposite: orthodoxy.

The term "orthodoxy" combines two Greek words that can be translated as "straight belief" or even "right worship." It stands in opposition to "heterodoxy," which means "other/chosen belief."

While the Church has a very clear definition of heresy, she does not precisely define orthodoxy. Indeed, the word is somewhat alien to Catholicism, appearing only once in the texts of the Second Vatican Council and never in the New Testament.

So, what is orthodoxy? Here's a useful definition from G. K Chesterton, the great English Catholic writer: "It means the Apostles' Creed, as understood by everybody calling himself Christian until a very short time ago, and the general historic conduct of those who held such a creed."[3]

Chesterton, writing in 1908, insisted that orthodoxy is a "flesh and blood" reality, not just an intellectual system.[4] In terms of the believer, orthodoxy happens when the fullness of God's Truth—the Person of Jesus Christ—becomes integrated with the believer's life.

Without this fusion of "right belief" and "right living" in and with the living Christ, orthodoxy can become a joyless catalogue of dogmas, always searching for heresies in our midst. Just as we must use the word "heresy" with great restraint, the same is true of "orthodoxy," especially when applying it to ourselves against anyone else.

---

[3] G. K. Chesterton, *Orthodoxy* (New York: John Lane Company, 1908), 20.
[4] Ibid., 21.

·· 7 ··

How should we fast?

Dear Father Kerper,
I struggle during the Lenten season, especially with the whole idea of fasting, which doesn't seem to mean much anymore. Local seafood restaurants fill up on Friday evenings with Catholics fulfilling their no-meat-on-Friday "sacrifice." Lobster and chowder just don't seem too much of a sacrifice to me. Aren't these people hypocrites?

Your question about Lenten fasting and lobster-eating Catholics opens the door to a much weightier question: How can an individual Catholic move from legalism to a life of true Christian penance?

Let's begin with legalism, the tendency to believe that one achieves salvation primarily by observing laws. For sure, obeying just and reasonable laws, such as Church rules about fasting and abstinence, is a good thing. Some people, however, want to stop there, observing the minimal requirement just to avoid punishment.

Obedience, of course, is not the problem. The real danger is a minimalist attitude that keeps a person from moving beyond mere external practices to a real change of heart. That's what God offers us: transformation. After all, Jesus came to give us abundant life, not an eternal parole from Hell.

God's Word, as expressed by both testaments, clearly commands penance, specifically fasting, but not exclusively as a nasty penalty or test. Its real purpose is to empty us of ourselves so that God can "fill the hole," so to speak.

The free act of reducing, or totally eliminating, the consumption of food also fosters true humility by making us vividly aware of our total dependence on God. This "transformative fasting" is what Moses, Elijah, John the Baptist, and other prophets did. Jesus Himself, of course, fasted frequently. Such fasting was never legalistic; rather it was always integral to a deeper mystical experience.

Unfortunately, religious legalism obscures the true meaning of fasting. In some Gospel texts Jesus confronts some opponents with the tension between the spirit and the law of fasting. As always, Jesus honors common religious practices while inviting people to a deeper spiritual experience.

Following the indisputable example of Jesus, Christians have practiced fasting from earliest times. Over the centuries, the Church has codified this penitential practice, sometimes with rigorous precision, at other times with liberality.

These specific Church regulations emphasize the value of fasting; they also foster unified penance by Catholics during Lent. But, as it was in the Lord's time, religious people continue to struggle with the letter and the spirit of fasting.

This brings us to the "Lobster on Lenten Friday" syndrome. Without doubt, a Catholic who abstains from meat on Friday and enjoys a seventy-five-dollar meal at an elegant seafood restaurant has observed Church law perfectly. But the spiritual dimension is entirely lost. The same applies to "Lenten weight-loss programs." Although dieting and fasting may both melt off ten or fifteen

How should we fast?

pounds, they have entirely different motives. The purpose of Lent is to come closer to God, not to lose weight.

Here's another point to consider: the lobster eater has completely missed the necessary connection between fasting and almsgiving. In ancient Israel, food not consumed by fasting people rightly belonged to the poor, those on a "permanent fast." Fasting, thus, drew people closer to one another by allowing the well fed to taste the hunger of the poor, and the poor to enjoy the food of the rich. In a small way, fasting promotes social justice.

By the way, the universal Church still designates every Friday, not just Lenten Fridays, as penitential days. And Church law specifically identifies abstinence from meat as the preferred act of penance.

Current Church law allows each national conference of bishops "to substitute other forms of penance, especially works of charity and exercises of piety" for fasting and abstinence. Since 1966 the bishops of the United States have asked Catholics to select their own Friday penitential practices, one of which remains fasting and abstinence. Contrary to what many think, the Church never abolished mandatory penance on Fridays. We are all obligated to do something.

You also asked whether the lobster-eating Catholics are hypocrites. We shouldn't jump to that conclusion. Instead, we should recognize that many Catholics, myself included, are "works in progress," content to do the minimum until guided to a deeper understanding of religious observance.

·· 8 ··
Are we required to give to everyone who asks for something?

Dear Father Kerper,
In the Gospels, Jesus seems to demand that we give money to every beggar who comes along. Should we take His words literally? I'm not rich, and some of these people hit me for a donation whenever I walk down the street. I feel guilty when I don't give them anything. Am I sinning by not responding to their appeal?

In a wonderful way, your question reveals your own basic goodness. You have listened carefully to the words of Jesus, and you acknowledge that His words lay claim to your whole life, including your dealings with people in need. You also experience the tension between the Lord's seemingly impossible demands and your own limited resources.

Let's begin with the matter of taking the words of Jesus literally. The Gospels do indeed tell us that Jesus said things like: "Give to every one who begs from you; and of him who takes away your goods do not ask them again" (Luke 6:30) and "Sell your possessions, and give alms" (Luke 12:33).

Also, the requirement to assist the poor is powerfully reinforced by two of Jesus' parables.

The first is the Lord's depiction of the last judgment (Matt. 25:31-46). Here, Jesus states that the sole criterion for salvation or damnation is a person's response to the hungry, the needy, the grieving, and so on. His words are sharp: "Truly, I say to you, as you did it not to one of the least of these, you did it not to me" (Matt. 25:45).

The second is the parable of Lazarus and the rich man (Luke 16:19-31). Jesus paints a terrifying picture of a man condemned forever, apparently because of a single sin: neglect of one poor man in need.

These passages, especially when combined with numerous other texts in both testaments, clearly teach us that every believer must give freely to the needy. This is a nonnegotiable, although often overlooked, requirement of the Gospel. Why?

Jesus forcefully insists on almsgiving as a means of changing our vision of other people and ourselves. In fact, true conversion means changing one's entire outlook on reality.

When Christians freely give alms to a stranger, they see the person, no matter how unattractive, as a living image of Christ. This happens through the mystery of the Incarnation, the unity of divinity and humanity in the person of Jesus Christ. Because humanity has an essential unity, everyone—regardless of belief or moral condition—has some connection with Christ. The act of almsgiving, then, acknowledges and honors Christ within the other.

Almsgiving also changes our self-image by allowing us to see ourselves as "Godlike." Perhaps this sounds blasphemous, but

Are we required to give to everyone?

various biblical passages make the same point. Here's just one: "You must therefore set no bounds to your love, just as your heavenly Father sets none on his" (see Matt. 5:48). To put it another way, by giving to the poor, especially to one person, we activate our God-given power to reflect God's own generous love in the world.

Now, to practical matters. You ask whether a Christian must literally follow the Lord's command "to give to all who ask."

Here we must move beyond specific situations to general patterns of behavior. Considering the biblical passages cited, especially Matthew 25 and the Lazarus parable, one must conclude that some sort of personal assistance to people in need is absolutely required. How one does this is another matter.

Some people — say, Mother Teresa or Dorothy Day of the Catholic Worker movement — discern a special vocation from God to deal with poor and broken people in a face-to-face way. People like them do heroic work and manifest God's generosity in an especially luminous way. But what about everyone else?

To find that answer for yourself, I would suggest that you examine your finances and personal time. Ask yourself these questions:

+ What portion of my income goes to charity? Here I would include not only contributions to groups that help the poor, but also financial gifts to needy neighbors, relatives, coworkers, and even strangers on the street. Almsgiving that comes entirely from one's excess is nice, but true almsgiving should involve the diminishment and simplification of one's own lifestyle. For example, could I skip my three-dollar latte by giving the money to a beggar?

+ Some people excuse themselves from helping panhandlers by arguing that the money will be misused. Please remember that the Lord requires charitable acts, not effective social work. A gift given in love has great value even when bestowed upon a con artist.

+ Do I spend time with people in need? For sure, Jesus speaks of material help, but His main interest is not economic. It's personal. Every Christian needs a Lazarus, a person who can claim his attention and concern, not just his money. Such a person may be right in front of you. As Saint Teresa of Calcutta once said to a woman who wanted to share in her work, "My dear friend, Calcutta is in your own living room."[5]

You also asked about sin. Some sins are evil actions. Other sins are failures to be what God has empowered us to be. Regarding personal assistance to the poor, we sin tragically by failing to see Christ in the other and, perhaps worse, by failing to allow God's goodness to flow through us to the other.

---

[5] Mary Poplin, *Finding Calcutta: What Mother Teresa Taught Me about Meaningful Work and Service* (Downers Grove, IL: InterVarsity Press, 2008), 201.

9

What is the Act of Contrition? Why is it so important?

Dear Father Kerper,
In one of your letters the Act of Contrition came up in the question and in your answer. I'm embarrassed to say that I have no idea what the Act of Contrition is. What is it, and why is it so important?

Please don't be embarrassed by asking. Your great question reminds me that at times priests use specialized terms and assume that everyone knows what they mean. So thank you for leading me to be clearer in these responses.

So, what is the Act of Contrition? On one level, it's a formal prayer recited during Confession, usually right before the priest says, "I absolve you from your sins, in the name of the Father, and of the Son, and of the Holy Spirit." In some settings, it may be prayed before or after Confession. And it can also be prayed apart from Confession, especially before going to bed.

Please understand, however, that the Act of Contrition is not primarily a magical formula rattled off thoughtlessly to guarantee instant forgiveness. Rather, it expresses in words a deeply personal *act* that engages a person's affections and will. The words, no matter how accurately they may be recited, do nothing without the act.

This act has three essential steps. We discover these by taking apart the most traditional form.

Step 1: Be sorry for your sins

"Contrition" comes from the Latin *contristare*, "to be with sadness." And so we begin the prayer by saying, "O my God, I am heartily sorry for having offended You." Here we express to God our *feeling* of sadness that flows from our honest acknowledgment of sin. This sorrow, which is an emotion rooted in the heart, is the first step toward forgiveness. Indeed, without this emotional response to offending God, we would never bother to confess our sins at all.

The prayer mentions two types of sorrow. This first is based on fear. We say, "Because of Your just punishments." The second arises from genuine love of the Lord. We say, "Because [my sins] offend You, my God, whom I should love above all things." Classical Catholic theology called the first type "imperfect contrition" and the second type "perfect contrition." Although we should always try to stir up genuine sorrow motivated solely by our love of God, the sadness that comes from fear of punishment and recognition of the foolishness of sin is sufficient to turn us to the Lord, who longs to forgive us.

Step 2: Renounce sin

After expressing our sorrow, we then turn against sin itself by saying, "And I detest all my sins." This hatred of sin is absolutely necessary

What is the Act of Contrition?

because the love of God cannot coexist with any lingering "love" of sin, even the slightest. In other words, no one can strike a cozy compromise between God and sin, trying to keep both as part of one's life. This, of course, doesn't mean that all sin will disappear instantly. It won't. Rather, although sin may persist, we must always disdain and resist it. This bring us to the most difficult step.

Step 3: Resolve to amend your life

Every authentic Act of Contrition must include a solemn promise to stop sinning. The traditional form has these words: "I firmly resolve with the help of Your grace to sin no more and to avoid the near occasions of sin." Many people, of course, balk at this promise, pleading, "I am only human and will inevitably sin again. Should I still make such a promise?" Yes.

This promise sets one's will firmly against sin. As such, it represents a free and conscious turning away from sin and toward God. This reaffirmation of one's basic commitment to God is essential. Without it, a person forever straddles the fence between God and sin. Even worse, confessing a sin while planning to commit it again blocks God's forgiveness. This reduces the sacrament of Penance to a "license to sin." Some people, unfortunately, ensnare themselves in a pattern of serious sin followed by Confession, then they repeat the sin, go to Confession again, and so on. This usually means that the firm purpose of amendment is lacking and that the sinner has seriously misunderstood how the sacrament of Penance works.

Now, please note the phrase "to avoid the near occasions of sin." This is crucial for any strategy to keep the promise to stop sinning. The term "occasions of sin" refers to people, places, and things that we know result in sin. Examples abound: someone with a drinking problem should not go to cocktail parties; someone who gets furious about current affairs should not listen to radio talk shows; someone who has trouble with chastity should not have easy access to the Internet; someone who slanders other people should not sit with people who enjoy gossip.

As you can now see, the Act of Contrition is much more than a set prayer. In a true sense, it stands at the very center of Christian life, which began on the day of our Baptism. At that time our parents and godparents formally renounced sin on our behalf. In effect, they declared that sin and God's grace are completely incompatible. Whenever we say the Act of Contrition, we reaffirm that essential truth, express our sorrow for past sins, and declare our hope that God's grace will surely triumph within us.

PART II

The New Evangelization and Old Neighbors: Our Life in the World

·· 10 ··
What is God's name?

Dear Father Kerper,
Recently some people told me that the Catholic Church is against using God's real name, which in the Bible is Jehovah. In fact, they said that Pope Benedict recently banned Catholics from ever using this name. If this is God's true name, why prohibit it?

This question comes up fairly often. Actually, you raise three distinct but interconnected issues: first, the name Jehovah; second, the use of the name Yahweh in worship; and third, the possibility of a divine name.

Let's begin with the name Jehovah. If you search through any relatively recent translation of the Bible, you won't find it. Why? Because almost all scholars agree that it is a mistranslation of four Hebrew letters; it was rendered into our standard alphabet as YHWH or JHWH.

The origin of the name Jehovah

Here's what happened. As reverence for God's name deepened among the people of Israel, they stopped uttering YHWH. This happened around 300 BC. To remind readers not to say the revealed name, scribes began to insert the vowel points of *Adonai* (Hebrew for "Lord") above the consonants YHWH. When people read the biblical text aloud they always substituted "Adonai/Lord" for "YHWH/God." Beginning in late medieval times, scholars who translated the Hebrew text into Latin and other European languages created the name Jehovah by mistakenly merging the four consonants—YHWH—with the vowel points of Adonai. Over the centuries, the pronunciation evolved into Jehovah.

There is still another huge problem with YHWH: no one really knows what it means. Most translators render Yahweh as "I am who am." Others prefer "I am who will be." And some even translate it simply as "Being." Also, some scholars even suggest that the ultimate fuzziness of YHWH means that God did not want to reveal the Name at all. By this interpretation, then, God was saying to Moses, "My name is none of your business."

Please remember that Jehovah's Witnesses have long disputed this standard account of the origin of "Jehovah," claiming that it is the only true name of God. However, the scholarship on this point is quite persuasive that this is not the case.

Why "Yahweh" is no longer heard

Now, let's look at Pope Benedict's "ban" on using God's "real name." In August 2008, the Holy See issued a directive regarding the use of "Yahweh" in sacred music and public prayer. Two reasons were given:

First, Christians have never used this name to address God in public worship. Indeed, "Yahweh" first appeared in Catholic hymns in the early 1970s. This happened largely through the influence of the Jerusalem Bible, whose English translation appeared in 1966.

What is God's name?

Many Catholic academics favored this innovative translation and some trendsetting hymn writers, such as Gregory Norbet, Dan Schutte, and the Saint Louis Jesuits, began using "Yahweh" instead of "Lord" and "God." "Yahweh," they believed, captured the "flavor" of the Hebrew Scriptures, especially the psalms.

From the start, however, some liturgy experts objected to using "Yahweh" in public worship. Some considered it untraditional while others appealed to practical considerations, namely, that many people have no idea that "Yahweh" and "God" are the same.

Second, the actual oral pronunciation of "Yahweh" is considered potentially offensive to Jewish people. Recognizing the longstanding prohibition among Jewish people against uttering the Divine Name, some argued that Christians should not do what Jewish people consider objectionable, indeed, even sacrilegious.

God's true Name

Now, to the next big question: What is God's true name?

God, being infinite and beyond all human ideas, obviously surpasses any single name. The Bible expresses this essential truth by offering a rich variety of names and terms for God.

Let's start with "God," perhaps the most common name we use. Strictly speaking, this is not a name at all but a generic term, like "man" or "dog" or "ruler." It usually translates the Hebrew word *Elohim*, which is not really a personal name.

Hebrew Scriptures use other impersonal terms for God, such as "Lord," "Holy One," "Strong One of Jacob," "the Almighty," and so on. When the Jewish people translated the Hebrew Scriptures into Greek, they always replaced YHWH with the Greek work *kyrios*, which means "Lord." This Greek version circulated widely in the early Church. Hence, almost all early Christians would have addressed God as Lord, never Yahweh.

What about Jesus? Being a pious Jewish man, as He certainly was, Jesus would never have addressed God as Yahweh, at least not in public. Instead, He almost always used the term "Abba," which is the familiar form of "Father," equivalent to "Daddy" or "Papa." Note, too, that "Abba" is a title, not a divine name.

The only other term used by Jesus was *Eloi*, which means "God" in the generic sense. Jesus uttered this only once—shortly before dying on the Cross. Similarly, Saint Paul and other New Testament writers use "Father" and "God," never "Yahweh" or "Jehovah."

When people become overly concerned about retrieving the "true" Name of God, they overlook the loving nature of God. Because God truly loves us, it is safe to assume that God hears all sincere prayer regardless of what name a person may use. Indeed, genuine prayer may invoke no name at all. After all, a loving parent who hears the cries of a distressed child does not quibble about the child's use of the word "Mommy," "Mother," "Daddy," "Father," or whatever. The parent simply responds in love.

Do Christians and Muslims pray to the same God?

Catholics believe that Allah and the God we worship is indeed the same God. The *Catechism of the Catholic Church* states: "The plan of salvation also includes those who acknowledge the Creator, in the first place amongst whom are the Muslims; these profess to hold the faith of Abraham, and together with us they adore the one merciful God, mankind's judge on the last day" (no. 841).

Moreover, please note that the Catholic bishops of Malaysia went to court in 2009 when the Islamic government prohibited

What is God's name?

a Catholic newspaper from using the word "Allah" for God. The bishops argued that this prohibition violated their religious freedom because the state was interfering with Catholic worship, whose liturgical texts used "Allah" for God.

But how can Christians and Muslims use the same name for God when Christianity and Islam are so different?

To escape this apparent quandary, we need to distinguish between the generic "name" God and the many personal names attached to the Divine.

Contrary to widespread belief, "Allah" is not Islam's personal name for God. Rather, "Allah" is a contraction of two Arabic words: *al-ilah*, which mean "the deity." As such, Allah is not a proper name but rather a nameless term. To put it another ways, "Allah" is simply the Arabic equivalent of *Theos* in Greek, *Deus* in Latin, *El* in Hebrew, and *God* in English. These are all terms, not names.

When believing monotheists—whether Christian, Muslim, or Jewish—pray to God in whatever language they use, the prayers of all terminate at the same point: the one true God. How could it be otherwise? There is no other God.

Although all monotheists pray to the same God, this does not mean that we share the same religion, not at all. Believers in Judaism and Islam regard Christians as profoundly mistaken about the nature and identity of Jesus Christ. Both of these religions, precisely in defending strict monotheism, reject the Christian doctrines of the Trinity and the Incarnation, the teaching that Christ is a Divine Person with a human and a divine nature. Indeed, some even regard Christians as polytheists who believe in and worship three separate gods: Father, Son, and Holy Spirit. Of course, we aren't polytheists, but we appear to be so, especially to Muslims.

Despite wars, violence, and mutual persecutions through the centuries, the Church has always recognized an essential monotheistic kinship with Jewish and Muslim people. We find this delicately expressed in the prayers offered on Good Friday, which express hope and trust in the infinite wisdom of God, who listens patiently to every voice raised to His ears.

·· 11 ··
Why can't women be priests?

> Dear Father Kerper,
> I became very upset when I read that the Church has excommunicated a woman who had herself ordained as a priest. Why is this woman being singled out when other people, even priests, have done worse things? One person, writing in a local newspaper, said she was excommunicated for following her conscience. He cited the words of Cardinal Newman, who is on the way to sainthood, "Conscience first; the pope second." How can anyone defend excommunicating a good woman who wants to serve the Lord?

Many Catholics share your concern about what appears to be unfairness, discrimination against women, and the Church's violation of conscience. By raising this matter, you display a commendable passion for justice. The quest for justice, however, always requires clarity about the situation. The thought and life of Blessed John Henry Newman, whose famous quote you shared, offer valuable guidance here.

Let's begin with conscience. Cardinal Newman did indeed write: "I shall drink—to the pope, if you please—still, to Conscience first, and to the pope afterwards."[6] These words appear at the very end of Newman's long letter to the Duke of Norfolk written in 1870.

Newman firmly asserted that Catholics have no obligation to follow the pope's direction on matters beyond the realm of doctrine and morality. For example, Newman said that if the pope ever mandated that religious communities must establish lotteries, a priest who truly believed that gambling is wrong must disobey the order. Why? Because papal directives about fund-raising techniques are not free from error.[7]

For Newman, conscience is not the same as one's personal opinions about essential Catholic beliefs. Indeed, in his 1870 letter, he warned against "counterfeit" forms of conscience that "boast of being above all religions and to be the impartial critic of each of them."[8] Instead, he offered this definition: "[Conscience] is a messenger from [God], who, both in nature and in grace, speaks to us behind a veil, and teaches and rules us by His representatives. Conscience is the aboriginal Vicar of Christ."[9]

For a Catholic, conscience and essential Church teaching should operate together. As such, the conscience of a Catholic can never require a person to do what is wrong, contrary to the Faith, or impossible. On the matter of priestly ordination, no one—whether man or woman—can ever claim that his or her conscience absolutely

---

[6] Blessed John Henry Newman, *A Letter Addressed to the Duke of Norfolk* (London: Aeterna Press, 2015), Kindle ed.

[7] Ibid.

[8] Ibid.

[9] Ibid.

Why can't women be priests?

requires ordination, which is no one's right. By contrast, conscience would require a man to refuse ordination if he sincerely believed he had no vocation. A bishop would violate a man's conscience by commanding ordination.

In short, Newman's thought reduced to a bumper sticker should read: "Conscience first; the pope second—in everything that's not his proper business." When the pope, in communion with Catholic bishops everywhere, simply reasserts established teaching about the priesthood, he minds his "proper business."[10]

Now, let's consider the excommunication of "ordained women." Excommunication does not necessarily imply that a person has sinned. Rather excommunication occurs when a person acts or believes in ways that directly contradict the Church's own self-understanding and structures.

As to ordination, anyone—regardless of gender—who attempts to receive Holy Orders, whether validly or not, from anyone other than a Catholic bishop in full communion with the bishop of Rome incurs excommunication. In recent times, many more men than women have been excommunicated for unauthorized ordinations; hence the key issue is not gender discrimination.

Excommunication in these cases is not primarily a punishment but a way to ensure that Catholic people know who is—and who is not—a Roman Catholic priest. Permit me to use an analogy from the marketplace.

If Toyota began to put Ford emblems on their cars and sold them as Fords, they still wouldn't be Fords. If such a thing happened, Ford would be horribly remiss if it allowed Toyotas to be passed off as genuine Fords.

---

[10] Cf. Joseph Cardinal Ratzinger, *On Conscience* (San Francisco: Ignatius Press, 2007), Kindle ed.

Through excommunication the Church removes its "brand" from everyone — male and female — who circumvents the standard process for validating God's call to ordained ministry. Without this discipline, all sorts of people could claim that God had "called" them to the priesthood. No one would be able to sort out Roman Catholic priests from "independent Catholic" priests, a true contradiction of terms.

Now, let's turn to the matter of sincere people who can't be ordained in the Catholic Church: women because of the Church's teaching that only men can be ordained, and men who want to combine marriage with ordination, something blocked by canon law. How does a person follow his or her conscience?

Let's return to Cardinal Newman. For many years he experienced agonizing tension between his conscience and his "birth right" denomination, the Church of England. After long and faithful service as a devoted Anglican minister and scholar, he eventually admitted that his understanding of the Church had evolved from the Anglican to the Roman Catholic version. His tortured conscience forced him to conclude that he could no longer hold pastoral office in the Anglican Church because he had become fully Roman Catholic in theology and spirituality.

Being a man of impeccable integrity, Newman believed it was impossible to cling to his Anglican pulpit and parsonage, all the while pleading that his conscience had dictated that he preach and teach Roman Catholicism. He left the Church of England and became a Roman Catholic, a courageous move that cost him dearly. Among other things, he lost pastoral employment, the right to teach in the university, and many cherished friends.

Newman clearly understood that the "doctrinal boundaries" of Catholicism are not infinitely elastic, especially teachings and practices that the Church firmly believes reflect the will of Christ.

Why can't women be priests?

This is the root of the Catholic position about the ordination of women.

In 1994, Pope John Paul II put it this way: "I declare that the Church has no authority whatsoever to confer priestly ordination on women and that this judgment is to be definitively held by all the Church's faithful."[11] Here, John Paul II did not express his personal opinion. Rather, his statement validated centuries of universal belief and practice, not only among Catholics but also among the Orthodox Churches.

The fixation on priestly ordination often blinds us to the diverse forms of ministry within the Catholic Church. Currently, hundreds of devoted, skilled, and creative women serve in full-time ministry in our diocese. And through the centuries, the vast majority of vowed religious have been women. These women have served the Lord and His people very well, always following their consciences in pursuit of the possible.

---

[11] Saint John Paul II, apostolic letter *Ordinatio Sacerdotalis* (On Reserving Priestly Ordination to Men Alone) (May 22, 1994), no. 4.

·· 12 ··

Why doesn't Pope Francis like pets?

Dear Father Kerper,
I like Pope Francis but am somewhat annoyed by his comments about people giving too much attention to their pets. I mean, he took the name Francis, who loved animals so much. Why is he so down on pets?

Pope Francis is definitely not criticizing people for having pets. Not at all. Rather, the Holy Father's comments, which seem negative, accurately reflect the views of Saint Francis, whose own approach to animals differs from today's tendency to elevate animals above people.

We learn about the approach of Saint Francis primarily from Saint Bonaventure (1221-1274), the greatest of all Franciscan theologians. His *Life of Saint Francis* has a chapter entitled "On His Affectionate Piety and How Irrational Creatures Were Affectionate toward Him." Saint Bonaventure wrote that Saint Francis loved animals mainly because they reminded him of God, their true origin, not because of cuteness or friendliness toward humans. For

Saint Francis, animals were "sacramentals," whose mere existence innocently and unconsciously pointed toward God.

Saint Bonaventure put it this way: "When [Saint Francis] considered the primordial source of all things, he was filled with even more abundant piety, calling creatures, no matter how small, by the name of brother and sister, because he knew they had the same source as himself."[12]

Saint Francis, according to his saintly biographer, had a special love for lambs. Whenever he saw a little lamb he immediately thought of Christ, the Lamb of God sacrificed for the salvation of all humanity. Seeing a lamb inevitably became an inspiration for prayer and contemplation. His love for lambs was so intense that Saint Francis once cursed a vicious old sow who killed a newborn lamb. After grieving for the dead lamb, Saint Francis said, "Alas, brother lamb, innocent animal, you represent Christ to me. A curse on that impious beast that killed you; may no man or beast ever eat of her!"[13] Saint Bonaventure reported that the sow died three days later after an excruciating illness. Even Saint Francis had favorites—and disliked nasty animals.

Although the patron saint of pets, Saint Francis never kept animals as personal possessions; his strict vow of poverty precluded ownership of anything, including pets. Saint Bonaventure noted that people often presented animals to Saint Francis as gifts. After spending some time with them, Saint Francis inevitably encouraged them to return to their natural habitat.

---

[12] Ilia Delio, *Simply Bonaventure: An Introduction to His Life, Thought, and Writings* (New York: New City Press, 2001), 148.

[13] *Bonaventure: The Soul's Journey into God, the Tree of Life, the Life of Saint Francis*, ed. Ewert Cousins (Mahwah, NJ: Paulist Press, 1978), 255.

Why doesn't Pope Francis like pets?

Saint Bonaventure recounted the touching story of a captured wild rabbit presented to Saint Francis by an admirer, perhaps as a potential entrée for dinner. After his friend had departed, Saint Francis spoke to the rabbit, warning it not to become ensnared by hunters again. He then turned the rabbit loose, but amazingly the rabbit kept returning to Saint Francis, who, Saint Bonaventure says, "fondled it with warm affection and seemed to pity it like a mother." Finally, Saint Francis enlisted some friars to take the rabbit far away so that he could live freely and be unable to seek out Saint Francis again. The rabbit lived out its life in freedom and peace.

In keeping with authentic Franciscan spirituality, which Pope Francis certainly shares, we must always respect and cherish animals, large and small, cute and ugly, as wondrous reflections of God's loving and creative power. But we must also recognize that our responsibility to human beings, who are created in God's image and likeness, always trumps our concern for any animals, who are only faint reflections of God's glory. This is the message of the Holy Father—and Saint Francis.

·· 13 ··

Can a non-Catholic be a godparent for my child?

Dear Father Kerper,
Six months ago, my wife and I had our first child. I wanted my best friend to be the godfather. The priest told us that this wasn't permitted because my friend is a Lutheran. This seems like discrimination. I also know that priests have allowed Protestants to be godparents. I don't get it. The Church's rules seem arbitrary and unfair.

Congratulations! Seeing new life, especially a firstborn child, causes many parents to think deeply about spiritual matters. The tension around the selection of your child's godfather can open the door to a richer understanding of these essential connections.

Let's begin by putting aside some popular ideas about godparents. The godparent is not a "replacement parent." Some believe that godparents get custody of godchildren if their parents die. Others designate godparents as a way of honoring close friends or favorite relatives. By asking someone to serve as a godparent, a parent manifests trust and esteem. Some also hope to secure a permanent relationship with a friend by formally linking the friend to the godchild.

I suspect you chose your friend as godfather because of friendship and your desire to honor him. These are noble motives, but the role of godparent is not about friendship or good personal example. Rather, the godparent agrees to exercise an office on behalf of the parents and the Catholic Church. Is this religious discrimination?

Civil law recognizes discrimination in employment, housing, banking and so forth. Religious discrimination is wrong also, but not necessarily in matters involving religion itself. It's one thing to refuse to rent your apartment to Lutherans just because they're Lutherans. It's quite another thing to insist that godparents be Roman Catholics. In the first, religion is irrelevant; in the second, it's crucial.

For example, candidates for ordination must be baptized and confirmed Catholics. Here we have a positive distinction favoring Catholics and excluding others. No reasonable person would regard this Church law as anti-Protestant. Just as the priest receives an office, so too does the godparent.

The *Catechism of the Catholic Church* teaches that godparents "must be firm believers, able and ready to help the newly baptized on the road of Christian life." To fulfill such a task, one must hold the beliefs of the Catholic Church and live by them.

Let's say that you hope your daughter will excel at tennis. Imagine that she has such prodigious skill in the sport that you seek a private coach. Surely, you would hire a tennis coach, not a swimming coach. Imagine a swimming coach trying to teach tennis! Perhaps an excellent swimming coach could help her with physical

Can a non-Catholic be a godparent for my child?

training, general athletic principles, and sportsmanship, but not the specifics of tennis.

A godparent is much like a coach. Just as it's unfair to ask a superb swimmer to coach tennis, it's equally unfair to ask someone who is not a committed Catholic to share in the spiritual coaching of a Catholic child. Moreover, it puts the non-Catholic in the awkward position of participating publicly in Catholic rituals, specifically the child's Baptism, First Communion, and Confirmation. Think of how uncomfortable it would be for a committed Lutheran, whose beliefs about the Eucharist differ from ours, to share in your daughter's First Communion celebration.

Your good friend may have an enormously positive influence on your daughter's character and spirituality. He's not, however, equipped to "coach" her in the specifically Catholic form of Christian faith.

You also bring up the point that you have encountered priests who allow non-Catholics to serve as godparents. We need to refine our terms here. The Church does indeed allow baptized non-Catholics to act as Christian witnesses. Apart from witnessing the event, they have no religious responsibilities toward the child. Although often called godparents, they really aren't. Every baptized person needs at least one baptized and confirmed Catholic godparent. Hence, one can never have two Christian witnesses.

At first glance, some Church disciplines, such as the ones about godparents, seem unreasonable. However, a careful examination usually shows that such practices make sense. They can guide people to what's truly good for everyone involved — children, parents, godparents, and the whole community of faith.

·· 14 ··

Why can't we have a Catholic wedding at our favorite inn?

Dear Father Kerper,
My fiancé and I want a full Catholic wedding. Both of us grew up near a lake and want to have the wedding at an inn nearby, but we've been told that we can't! A friend of mine, who is Catholic, and her nonreligious fiancé had their wedding at a restaurant. This seems unfair?

I understand your frustration about your wedding plans, and I admire your desire to receive the sacrament of Matrimony rather than a "civil bond." Perhaps what follows will help you and your fiancé to arrange a celebration that harmonizes the Church's requirements with your desire to have a wedding that is truly personal. Tensions like yours often arise because the Church's understanding of what happens at a wedding differs from popular beliefs.

You mentioned your desire to have a wedding that has "personal meaning," particularly the actual location of the event, such as the inn where you and your fiancé first met. While that location has enormous personal significance for you, we must always remember that a Catholic wedding is an act of public worship, not a private ceremony.

Consider what happens at a Catholic wedding. Two people, already united with Christ and one another through Baptism, come before a priest or deacon and a community of fellow believers. In the presence of this "miniature Church," they exchange the sacred vows of Matrimony. Through these acts of mutual consent, each spouse bestows on the other the sacrament of Matrimony.

The exchange of vows is a very holy and powerful event. Moreover, it involves three parties: bride, groom, and Christ. Because Christ is the preeminent partner of the marriage—the foundation—the principal focus of the ceremony falls on Him, not on the couple.

In light of the "Christ focus" of the wedding, the Church insists that the ceremony ordinarily happen within a church building. Because Christ is the center of the event, it makes perfect sense to have it happen within His "house," not on a beach or in a ballroom. After all, Christ is the most honored wedding guest, in the form of his sacramental Presence.

This, of course, does not make the wedding "impersonal." Indeed, the Church law brings out the "personal" aspect of the wedding by urging couples to celebrate it in their own church. The old *Code of Canon Law* (1917) actually required that weddings happen within the bride's church. Current church law allows the wedding to occur within the groom's church, and, with proper permission, in any Catholic church.

The Church's clear preference for weddings within familiar churches is meant to stress the interconnection among all sacraments. For example, years ago many brides celebrated their weddings

Why can't we have a Catholic wedding at an inn?

in the churches where they had received Baptism, Confirmation, and First Communion. In those cases, the spiritual connection was abundantly clear. Now, of course, the mobility of families makes this somewhat rare. However, it is praiseworthy—and beautiful—to have your wedding in the place where you regularly partake of the Eucharist. After all, your "spiritual home" is your true home and the venue of the most personal events of your life: your living relationship with the Lord.

Now, let's consider the "unfairness" of the Church's recognition of your friend's marriage to a non-Catholic, which took place at a restaurant. Such "non-church" weddings do indeed happen, although very rarely. Bishops can grant "dispensations from place" when the non-Catholic party has some genuine aversion to having a ceremony within a Catholic church. At times, these dispensations are granted to accommodate the sensitivities of family members of the non-Catholic party.

In these rare cases, the Church graciously suspends the normal requirements in the interest of the spiritual welfare of the couple. To put it another way, the Church does everything possible to enable the Catholic party to contract a valid marriage. The matter of location, although very important, is less important than the marriage itself. Hence, the requirement that weddings happen in a church is not absolute.

With proper planning and spiritual preparation, I'm confident that you will have a wedding that is both personal and in full accord with Church law. More important, you will have a happy and holy marriage that began in the "house" of the "third party"—Christ Himself.

·· 15 ··

How do I explain about receiving Communion to my non-Catholic relatives?

Dear Father Kerper,
My family is coming over for Christmas Eve and we traditionally go to Mass that evening. How do I explain to family members who are not Catholic that they can't receive Holy Communion? I also have some Catholic family members who I think are not properly prepared for Holy Communion. Should I speak to them? And what can I say?

Your concern about your Christmas Eve situation involves two considerations: social etiquette and theology. By keeping these distinct from one another, perhaps you can avoid hurting anyone's feelings while affirming Catholic teaching and practice.

Let's begin with social etiquette. People who have good manners usually understand the mutual rights and obligations of hosts and guests. Following the norms of Christian hospitality, especially as promoted by Saint Benedict, hosts should always welcome, honor, serve, and accommodate the special needs of guests. In response, guests should always respect the host and follow the household rules. Some rules are obvious: no smoking at meals, no feet on the coffee table, no speaking about embarrassing subjects, and so on.

Today, one cannot presume that everyone knows or accepts the household rules. Hence, the host may need to review the rules in a gentle and discreet way. One may reasonably expect—or at least hope—that guests will honor the host's generous hospitality by following the most important household rules. This certainly applies to "church etiquette," especially the norms pertaining to reception of Holy Communion.

Since almost all Christian denominations practice "open communion," which means that everyone partakes of communion regardless of their beliefs or religious affiliations, many people assume that Catholics do the same. This happens because many Christians regard their "communion services" primarily as "fellowship meals" that somehow manifest shared friendship among the participants, including those who may have no settled religious beliefs. As such, many Christians view the Catholic policy about "intercommunion" as a grievous violation of hospitality in that Catholics do not share their "food," thereby apparently judging others as unworthy of Holy Communion. While this response is understandable, it misses the well-founded and biblically based theological reasons for long-standing Catholic—and Orthodox—practice.

A delicate conversation with your guests could proceed in the following way.

Begin with a preview of the parts and the flow of the Mass. You could show them a missalette or a hymnal and mention the possibility of singing, making the responses, and so on. When you get to the Communion Rite, you may acknowledge the common practice of "intercommunion" among most other Christians. Next,

How do I explain about receiving Communion?

mention that Christians have learned to pray and work together while tolerating doctrinal and liturgical differences, including very different understandings about the Eucharist. Then mention that Catholics reasonably assume that other Christians will respect long-standing Catholic practice without feeling hurt.

Stating Catholic practice, which many Christians reject, is never sufficient. It must be explained in a careful, sensitive, and theologically correct way. Here's what you could say: "Catholics see the reception of Holy Communion as the clearest way of identifying themselves publicly as people who fully accept and live according to Catholic beliefs. I know that you have some sincere beliefs that differ from ours, and that you would not want to be identified as a Catholic. We're very happy that you will worship with us at Christmas, but we don't want you to violate your own religious identity by doing something that only Catholics will do."

This explanation moves the discussion beyond social etiquette to theology. It stresses the genuine Catholic desire to protect the religious integrity of Christians who do not accept Catholic teaching about the Eucharist, Church authority, marriage, and a vast range of other issues. Most important, it doesn't propose our Catholic practice as an arbitrary penalty imposed upon "outsiders" for being grave sinners, heretics, or schismatics.

If a visitor is genuinely respectful and open-minded toward the position of the Catholic Church, there should be no anger or hurt feelings. After all, polite guests respect the peculiar practices and customs of other people when they visit their homes and places of worship. Why should anyone who visits a Catholic church feel hurt or angry if Catholics follow their long-standing beliefs at Christmas Eve Mass?

Now, let's consider baptized Catholics who rarely worship, who were never fully instructed, or who have wandered into confusing spiritual territory. We all know such people. What should we do if they intend to receive Holy Communion? Here we must recognize our own severe limitations regarding knowledge and authority.

As to knowledge, no one can fully and accurately grasp the spiritual situation of another person. For example, we may consider someone "lapsed" or "irregular" when in fact he or she may have gone to confession, been fully reconciled with the Church, or embarked on a slow and complex spiritual journey that remains unfinished. In such cases, an untimely rigoristic or overzealous "instruction" may do more harm than good.

While bishops have the authority to declare that a specific Catholic should not receive Holy Communion, we do not. As faithful Catholics, we have the duty to speak prudently to people about Church teachings and practice, always hoping that they will respond properly. But we have no authority whatsoever to insist that people follow our personal judgments about their readiness to receive Holy Communion.

We must always remember that the work of conversion of hearts ultimately belongs to God, who often moves slowly and mysteriously. At most, we serve only as His humble and trusting partners. All success comes from Him.

Thanks for preparing well in advance to welcome your guests to Christmas Eve Mass. I trust that your kindness and reflection about these complicated matters will produce some small "fruits of unity" rather than division.

PART III

Baptize, Marry, and Bury: Our Life in the World to Come

16

Who can receive Last Rites?

Dear Father Kerper,
When my grandmother died in a nursing home late at night, we couldn't find a priest to give her Last Rites. In the morning, we finally got a priest, but he said he couldn't give Last Rites because she was already dead. Why not? I always thought Last Rites were for the dead.

I'm sorry that your grandmother passed into eternal life without receiving the Sacrament of the Sick and the prayers that a priest could have offered for her as she approached the moment of death. However, don't underestimate the value of your own prayers and your faithful presence at her bedside. Under the circumstances, you did something very good; and we must trust that everything done in love and faith will produce fruit in ways we may never know.

The priest was correct: only a living person can receive a sacrament. The problem here is the misleading term "Last Rites." Unfortunately, many people continue to believe that the Catholic Church has some sort of last sacrament or sacrament for the dead.

Strictly speaking, we don't. Indeed, we've never had such a thing. So how did we get the term "Last Rites"?

This popular term emerged from an incomplete translation of the official Latin text of the old Roman Ritual. The Latin form of the 1964 Roman Ritual had a section labeled *Ritus continnuus infirmum muniendi sacramentis extremis*. The English translation is: "The last rites as given without interruption." However, the Latin never used the term "Last Rites." Moreover, the English translation omitted the key Latin words that mean "for the fortifying/strengthening of the sick." The Latin text said nothing at all about death or dying.

All the prayers in the *Ritus continuus* or Last Rites referred to the living person, not a corpse. Although some of the prayers mentioned the possibility of imminent death, they commended a living person to God's mercy. There was nothing like an "absolution" of a dead person.

The old Roman Ritual, as well as the revised one, grouped together three sacraments — not mere "rites" — in the *Ritus continuus*: Anointing of the Sick, Holy Communion, and Penance and Reconciliation. As such, there was no additional sacrament associated with death.

Even the old Roman Ritual presumed that these three sacraments would be celebrated separately over the course of a person's final illness. The *Ritus continuus* was meant primarily for emergency situations. This ritual combination was never to be the norm, but the exception.

Whereas in the past, the priest usually acted alone in celebrating the sacraments for the sick and dying, today many other people share in this highly important work. For sure, the Church reserves some parts of this work exclusively to priests. For example, only a priest (not a deacon or a lay chaplain) can provide the Sacrament

Who can receive Last Rites?

of the Sick and absolution, either after confession or conditionally (if a person is unconscious, unable to speak, or possibly already dead). Today, however, Holy Communion is usually brought by an extraordinary minister of Communion, rarely by a priest.

This team approach is not entirely new. Indeed, one found hints of it already in the old Roman Ritual. For example, the rubrics for a rite called "Recommendation of the Departing Soul to God" states: *Dicantur sequentes orationes,* which means "the following prayers are said." Note how the Ritual avoided limiting these prayers to the priest. It presumed that others could say them.

Spiritual care of the sick and dying was always meant to extend over a long period and involve the broader community, not just the priest.

Please don't ask for "Last Rites" but spiritual care for the living. That's what the Church gladly offers.

·· 17 ··

Can Catholics believe in reincarnation?

Dear Father Kerper,
Since the soul is the only part of the person that really matters, what's wrong with believing in reincarnation? What difference does it make whether the soul is in a man or a lion or a bird or just free? I can't find anything in the Bible that condemns reincarnation.

Thanks for asking about reincarnation, an issue that touches upon two key Christian beliefs: first, the very nature of the human person; and second, the resurrection of the dead.

To begin with, reincarnation is the belief that a soul can move from one physical body to another. According to some non-Christian religions, this movement from "higher" to "lower" life forms, say, from a Persian king to a mosquito, happens because one has done either good or evil, deserving reward or punishment. The particular body acquired by a soul somehow reflects the deeds of its past life. This process of moving from body to body can continue repeatedly until the soul gets sufficiently "purified" and eventually freed from bodily life, which is understood as a prison.

This dualistic understanding of the human person extends far beyond religious concerns and appears in various forms of philosophy, especially those deriving from Plato. Through the centuries, some key philosophers have defined the human person as a "spiritual entity" or "consciousness" with no lasting connection with a body. Such ideas, although long popular among some Christians, devalue the human body and distort the biblical understanding of the human person.

Now, let's take a look at Sacred Scripture. It's true that nothing in the Bible directly rejects reincarnation. However, you will discover a remarkably consistent depiction of the human person as a living union of spirit and matter, both being valuable and necessary.

In the Hebrew Scriptures, we immediately meet this understanding in Genesis. In chapter 2, the inspired writer shows God forming a human body from clay. Then God blows the divine breath into the body. Here God's act causes human life, which is simultaneously spiritual and material. God does not insert an independent soul into a material container. Rather, body and soul exist together. As such, the notion that the soul of Adam could somehow freely migrate to another body while remaining Adam is completely foreign to the text.

A look at Israel's understanding of the afterlife also shows an avoidance of any body-soul dualism. Take, for example, the description of Abraham's postdeath situation: "Abraham breathed his last and died in a good old age, an old man and full of years, and was gathered to his people" (Gen. 25:8). Here we have a very earthy image of the afterlife as a gathering of bodily human beings whose original relationships somehow endure.

More important, later texts clearly assert some sort of bodily resurrection of previously dead bodies. For a very graphic image,

Can Catholics believe in reincarnation?

look at chapter 37 of Ezekiel. This dramatic prophesy culminates when a collection of human skeletons came alive "and stood upon their feet, an exceedingly great host" (Ezek. 37:10). The point is clear: God will eventually restore—and transform—the unique relationship between a particular body and a particular soul.

Everything we read in the Scriptures about the body-soul unity of the human person and the eventual bodily resurrection receives ultimate validation in and through the life, death, and Resurrection of Christ. To begin with, the Son of God is not an independent spiritual entity implanted in a human body temporarily. The prologue of Saint John's Gospel makes this abundantly clear: "The Word became flesh and dwelt among us" (John 1:14). Note the key the phrase "became flesh," which means that the Son of God became fully and permanently human.

Because of the Incarnation of the Word, which means the union of humanity and divinity in the divine person of Christ, His Resurrection is not merely the survival of His soul. Rather, the Resurrection necessarily involves His whole person, which is also bodily. Without the body, the risen Christ would not be truly human. Moreover, the Gospels, especially John's, stress that the body of the risen Christ is the same body that suffered crucifixion.

What difference does this make for us? Lots. The New Testament tells us that Christ's Resurrection is a preview of our ultimate destiny. Two passages from Saint Paul show this: "For if we have been united with him in a death like his, we shall certainly be united with him in a resurrection like his" (Rom. 6:5), and "[he] will change our lowly body to be like his glorious body, by the power which enables him even to subject all things to himself" (Phil. 3:21).

This brings us to your statement: "The soul is the only part of the person that really matters."

True, we often forget our spiritual dimension. However, a person's specific body is crucial to his or her future identity. Indeed, we believe that our personal identity after death will extend the bodily existence we now have. In other words, at the time of our resurrection, we will rise in the identifiable—although transformed—bodies we have now, not in some new "container."

But how can this body-soul linkage survive the inevitable decomposition of the corpse? Ludwig Ott, the author of the classical theological handbook *Fundamentals of Catholic Dogma* (1954), explained it this way: "The identity must not be conceived in such a fashion that all material parts which at any time, or at a definite moment belonged to the earthly body, will be present in the body in the resurrection. As the human body always remains the same in spite of the constant changing of its constituent matter, it suffices for the preservation of the identity, if a relatively small share of the amount of the matter in the earthly body is contained in the body after resurrection."

Take, for example, the case of Blessed John Henry Cardinal Newman. When his grave was opened with the intention of moving his body to a chapel for veneration, nothing was left. The sole bodily relic of Cardinal Newman is a single strand of hair! In a sense, that single hair can act as the seed of a risen body. God needs nothing more.

A simple line from Ludwig Wittgenstein, the great Austrian-British philosopher who lived from 1889 to 1951, serves to summarize: "The human body is the best picture of the human soul."[14] Because we each have a unique and unrepeatable soul, we also have just "one picture," the body we have now and in eternity.

---

[14] Ludwig Wittgenstein, *Philosophical Investigations*, trans. G.E.M. Anscombe (Upper Saddle River, NJ: Pearson Education, 1973), 178.

·· 18 ··
Is damnation real?

> Dear Father Kerper,
> If God loves everyone, how can anyone be damned to Hell forever? This seems to be the opposite of love. So, is damnation real? Do I have to believe in it?

Yes, damnation is real. Of course, many people, including some believing Christians, would like to suppress this troubling truth; but Sacred Scripture frequently and clearly asserts the real possibility of eternal loss. As such, damnation is an essential element of gospel truth and must be received as "good news." But how can any sane person regard damnation as good news?

The teaching about damnation is good news because it powerfully affirms the mystery of genuine human freedom, which undergirds the eternal durability of our moral choices. Let's now consider two key terms: "damnation" and "freedom."

When we hear the word "damnation" we usually cringe in horror, thinking of some type of devastating eternal punishment imposed on some poor soul by a vindictive and unforgiving God. Where's the love and mercy? How can this be? Doesn't damnation contradict everything we believe about God?

To begin with, we must note that the Greek New Testament has no single word that means "damnation." Usually we think of this as a judicial sentence, something like life in prison without death, a truly horrifying situation.

Older English versions of the New Testament, unfortunately, used the word "damnation" to translate four Greek words and phrases that actually mean "an irrevocable negative judgment of human behavior." Sometimes this was rendered as "condemnation."

By looking more closely at the Greek words, we begin to see something crucially important: "damnation" is not an arbitrary punishment inflicted on a sinner by God; rather, "damnation" is God's final evaluation and verification of a whole series of free moral choices made by a person through his or her lifetime. Because God always acts in an absolutely truthful way, He cannot render a favorable judgment for someone who lived in a gravely evil manner throughout his or her life and never repented.

Perhaps an example here will help us move beyond the abstract. If a high school student enrolls in algebra and then plays video games during class time, never studies, refuses to turn in homework assignments, gets a zero on the final exam, and then gets a big red F from the teacher, would anyone complain that the teacher had "damned" the poor student? Of course not! The big red F emerges directly from the student's freely chosen behavior. The teacher simply certifies that the failure has truly happened. Moreover, the student who flunks algebra can't—and shouldn't—move on to calculus, which is incomprehensible without grounding in algebra. The student—not the teacher—has closed the door to advancement in mathematics.

Here we see the interconnection between human freedom and judgment. Without genuine freedom, there's nothing to judge. Freedom here means the real possibility of making a choice for

Is damnation real?

good or evil without anything being predetermined or coerced. Please remember, God created human beings, not robots. Whereas people are capable of being good or evil, robots are not.

Now, the ultimate outcome of life—damnation or eternal life in the presence of God and the communion of saints—is vastly more important than how we do in school, but the same principle is at work. Our moral choices, which we freely make in and through God's grace, shape us as persons who are predominantly good or evil, either oriented completely toward love of God and neighbor or away from God and back into the isolated self.

In the end, damnation is God's definitive evaluation that a person has freely chosen to turn completely inward, thereby choosing to live alone within a self-constructed prison cell with no key.

T.S. Eliot, the great Anglo-Catholic poet and playwright, put it this way in his play *The Cocktail Party*: "What is hell? Hell is oneself. Hell is alone."[15]

Although God intensely desires eternal happiness for every human being, and extends mercy and forgiveness to everyone who asks, He also respects the freedom of people to choose radical forms of self-isolation, which obliterates every speck of love in their existence. To use the words of George Bernanos in his *Diary of a Country Priest*, "Hell means not to love anymore."[16] Because God is love, those who refuse to live in love exclude themselves from eternal life.

The big red F at the end of life—damnation—is scrawled in the handwriting of the damned, not of God. As that happens, God

---

[15] T. S. Eliot, *The Cocktail Party* (Harcourt, Brace and Company, 1950), 142.

[16] George Bernanos, *The Diary of a Country Priest* (Cambridge, MA: Da Capo Press, 2002), Kindle edition.

sadly assents to the free choice against love made by the person who was made for love, but a love born in true freedom, not coercion.

So, damnation is very real. And so is the glory and joy of eternal life. These two contrary possibilities verify the reality of the mystery of freedom. And that's the good news of damnation.

·· 19 ··

Whatever happened to Limbo?

Dear Father Kerper,
Last April, I heard that the Church had abolished Limbo. Years ago, my grandmother told me that nonbaptized babies go to Limbo instead of Heaven because of original sin. Now I hear that Limbo was just an opinion, not a Church teaching. How can I know what's really true and what's just opinion?

Thank you for your note of interest in this subject, which reflects your honest concern for the salvation of all of God's children. Yet I also realize that your question reflects the reality that some of us get very frustrated when ideas and practices suddenly change.

In order to answer your question we must distinguish doctrine from opinion based on what the Church calls the *hierarchy of truths*. This means that some teachings are more important than others.

Think of it this way. The owner's manual of your car will show you clearly how to turn on the engine, shift gears, and use the brake. Later, perhaps in a bad snowstorm, you'll learn how to use your defroster and rear window de-icer. Someday when you have nothing to do, you may even read about oil changes, tire pressure, and maintenance.

All these instructions are true and helpful, but each one is not equally important. You need to know where to put the key before you worry about tire pressure. Think of Church teaching as a spiritual owner's manual.

The Church has at least four markers for permanent teachings: Sacred Scripture, ancient creeds, council statements, and *ex cathedra* papal statements.

- ✛ First, Sacred Scripture expresses key beliefs, such as the oneness of God, the Trinity, the Incarnation, and the Resurrection of Christ.
- ✛ Second, ancient creeds, such as the Nicene and Apostles' Creeds, contain settled doctrines.
- ✛ Third, core doctrines of faith proposed by ecumenical councils are also permanent, although open to refinement, new formulations, and development.
- ✛ Fourth, teachings declared *ex cathedra* (from the chair) by the pope are unchangeable. So far, only two popes—Pius IX and Pius XII—have used this form of teaching.

Many older Catholics probably learned about Limbo in religion class. For years, Limbo was proposed as one possible way of resolving the apparent contradiction between two genuine Church teachings, namely, the necessity of Baptism for salvation and God's desire that everyone be saved.

As much as we want to know precisely what happens to nonbaptized persons—children and good people—the simple truth is that God's revelation doesn't tell us. In the past, Limbo became the favored opinion because many in the Church stressed the necessity of Baptism. Today, however, many theologians, including Pope Benedict XVI, see that opinion as explaining too much, thereby foreclosing possibilities known to God alone.

If you study Scripture and key Church documents you will find that nothing proposes Limbo as a settled and indisputable teaching. Indeed, it has none of the markers needed for permanent teachings.

Let's go back to the hierarchy of truths. God's revelation enlightens us only about matters essential for our salvation. Hence, God tells us how to live a good and moral life, confident that we come from Him, have been redeemed by Christ, and have the hope of eternal life. This information is like knowing how to switch on the engine and use the brake.

But God doesn't explain every detail of how His saving love works in the world. Such details are akin to a car's clock and DVD player. We can drive the car perfectly well without the correct time and music. Similarly, we can live the Christian life fully and joyfully without clear answers to every possible theological question.

One way of approaching this subject with those who have lost children through miscarriage, sickness, or even abortion is to reflect on God's mercy. The one consistent mystery of God that is found in all four markers of the truth is that God is not merely the God of justice, but also the God of mercy and love.

The point is to drive the car rather than to become too engrossed or even distracted by the owner's manual. And on our road to God, there must, and always will be, mysteries. Our challenge is to let those mysteries serve not as obstacles, but as opportunities for increasing our faith and desire to arrive at our destination, where, we are assured, all things will be revealed.

Can I baptize someone?

Every human being, even a nonbeliever, has the ability to baptize another person validly. However, the Church authorizes this only in cases of imminent death. A Catholic should therefore refrain from baptizing someone else's child, even a grandchild, and should not feel guilty about it. Such a situation calls for patient sensitivity toward the rights of the parents who have chosen not to baptize their child.

·· 20 ··
Is it okay to be cremated?

Dear Father Kerper,
Now that I'm getting older, I've started to think about prearranging my funeral. I've heard that the Church used to oppose cremation but now approves of it. I'm leaning toward cremation, mainly to save money on a grave, which seems like a waste. Also, I'd like my ashes scattered at Hampton Beach, where I spent many summers. Some Catholic friends have told me that sprinkling ashes is not allowed. Is this true? If so, why not?

I commend you for taking the time to plan your funeral. By making arrangements now, you have graciously relieved your loved ones of a very onerous—and often contentious—task. Now, let's walk through some issues.

Regarding cremation, you state that the Church "now approves of it." Strictly speaking, this is not correct. The Church merely tolerates cremation. Full body burial in consecrated ground remains the undisputed preference of the Church. The *Code of Canon Law*, which expresses the authentic "mind of the Church," says this: "The Church earnestly recommends that the pious custom of burying the bodies of the deceased be observed." As for cremation, the *Code* simply states: "The Church does not prohibit cremation unless it is chosen for reasons contrary to Christian doctrine" (cf. can. 1176.3).

The preference for burial, first declared in 1983, was strongly reinforced in an appendix pertaining to cremation in the 1997 *Order of Christian Funerals*. The rite maintains that cremation is permitted by the Church but it does not quite enjoy the same value as burial would, and the Church still urges that the body of the deceased be present for the funeral.

From earliest times, Christians have practiced full-body burial, a custom deeply rooted in the Jewish tradition of honoring the human remains of ancestors. Recall, for example, how the Israelites carried the bones of the patriarch Joseph with them as they fled from Egypt into the Sinai Desert (Exod. 13:19). Surely, if corpses didn't really matter, they wouldn't have taken the trouble to include Joseph's skeleton in their baggage.

By the time of Jesus, many Jews, notably the Pharisees, firmly believed in resurrection; hence, corpses were viewed as "seeds" of future bodily life. After Jesus' death and Resurrection, Christians viewed the burial of the dead as an imitation of Christ's entombment. Graves were blessed and venerated as the site of human remains destined for resurrection.

Knowing of their faith in resurrection, the enemies of Jews and Christians often cremated martyrs' remains as an additional punishment, as if to thwart their future life. It is interesting that a practice Christians now freely choose was once used to humiliate them. In fact, it was the denial of bodily resurrection that provoked the Church's prohibition against cremation. In the late nineteenth century, many enthusiastic proponents of cremation promoted it as an excellent way of repudiating Christian belief in bodily resurrection and the practice of venerating the saints. In response to the growing "cremation movement," the Catholic Church, in 1886,

Is it okay to be cremated?

officially prohibited Catholic membership in so-called cremation societies and refused funeral rites to anyone who deliberately chose cremation. This ban was included in the 1917 *Code of Canon Law*.

The prohibition was never absolute, however. Cremation has always been acceptable under certain circumstances, such as mass death caused by epidemics and wars. For example, victims of the black plague were burned in an attempt to prevent its further spread, and in this country in 1836, the corpses of the Mexican and Texan soldiers killed at the Alamo were all cremated. In 1963, the Church stated that cremation could be tolerated provided that there was no intention of denying bodily resurrection.

As for sprinkling your remains at the beach, here are some points to consider:

First, cremated remains, although not equivalent to a corpse, are still the residue of a human body. As such, they have a sacred quality, being the physical remnants of the temple of the Holy Spirit. They must be treated with respect.

Second, the burial place—whether a marked grave or a small plot holding an urn—is a blessed sacramental that reminds surviving loved ones of the inevitable resurrection of all human beings. Also, a burial site is a focal point of prayer and acts of remembrance by subsequent generations. If you toss your ashes into the ocean, your descendants, who may long to connect with your physical remains, will be deprived of a link with their past.

Some, of course, will object: "It's my body! I can dispose of it as I wish!" Not really. Ultimately, our bodies belong to God because they originate from God's creative power. We are not our own.

While the Church allows a lot of freedom in the arrangement of funerals and burials, our choices must always affirm the sanctity of the human body, even a dead one, and joyfully proclaim our belief in the bodily resurrection of the dead.

·· 21 ··

Do ghosts really exist?

Dear Father Kerper,
It seems as if there is a lot of evidence that there are ghosts that haunt people's homes. Do ghosts really exist?

Thanks very much for your question about the reality of ghosts. Some people, of course, would brush it off as a silly thing to ask, but it actually leads us to consider anew two key Christian beliefs: first, that every human person is a communion of body (matter) and soul (spirit); and second, that human life continues forever after bodily death, first as a bodiless soul, and eventually as a resurrected human being with body and soul reunited. To put your question differently: can these bodiless souls—ghosts—appear and intervene in our lives?

We have to clarify the term "ghost." I am not speaking here about menacing spirits that terrorize movie characters. This English word "ghost" comes from the German word "geist," which broadly means "spirit," including nonpersonal things such as the "spirit of the age" and so on. In English, "ghost" specifically means the soul of a dead person that becomes discernible through our eyes, ears, nose (some ghosts smell!), or skin.

In theory, billions of ghosts potentially exist because billions of human beings have "lost" their bodies through death. Strictly speaking, these disembodied souls are not ghosts because they have never become discernible to any living people. Only those few souls whose presence is seen or felt by others are truly ghosts. And their existence is plausible. But here we must proceed with great caution.

Let's look at Sacred Scripture. The book of Deuteronomy condemns anyone "who consults ghosts and spirits or seeks oracles from the dead" (see Deut. 18:10-11). And the book of Leviticus warn against using "mediums" to contact the souls of the dead (see Lev. 19:31; 20:6, 27). These legal prohibitions demonstrate that at least some people believed in ghosts. If they didn't, why prohibit attempted contacts?

The Old Testament also has a few ghost stories. The most famous one is in 1 Samuel 28:8-20. Here the inspired writer tells how King Saul met with the ghost of the prophet Samuel. In 2 Maccabees 15:1-16, you can read about the encounter between Judas Maccabeus, the great Jewish patriot, and the ghost of Onias, the dead high priest. These Old Testament laws and stories affirm that the people of Israel believed that human souls survive after death and can have contact with the living, at least occasionally.

Now, let's see what theology contributes to the matter. To be frank, many theologians haven't written much about ghosts, but some have, notably Saint Augustine and Saint Thomas Aquinas.

According to Saint Thomas, the souls of the dead who are in heaven can indeed manifest themselves to the living on their own initiative. Such appearances, however, are not "hauntings" meant to terrify or tease people. Rather, these saintly apparitions occur only to bring comfort and encouragement, never fear.[17] And

---

[17] Saint Thomas Aquinas, *Summa Theologica*, Suppl., Q. 69, art. 3.

remember, "saint" means anyone who dwells with God, not just those officially declared "saints" by the Church. In light of this, it is theoretically possible for loved ones, such as deceased grandparents or children (even babies), to become sensibly discernible to us. While such occurrences may be rare, there is no reason to rule them out. In a sense, these spirits are "ghosts" but they are benign, even loving.

Now we move to the matter of malicious ghosts, the nasty type that pop up in horror movies and novels. Saint Thomas clearly states that the souls of the dead, who are not in heaven, can never appear to the living without God's consent. But why would God ever allow ghosts to "haunt" people?

Saint Thomas gives two reasons: first, as a warning; and second, to seek spiritual assistance from the living in the form of prayer or good deeds to advance the dead person toward fulfillment in God. The ghosts or "non-saints" may annoy people, but they can never harm them.[18]

Of course, one can read somewhat credible stories about destructive "hauntings," but Saint Thomas always insisted that these "ghosts" were definitely not the souls of dead people, but something else, most likely demons masquerading as ghosts.[19]

This brief exploration about ghosts leads us to a very positive point: the spiritual bonds between the living and dead, especially those who love one another, are deep, unbreakable, and mysterious because they are rooted in the Body of Christ, which embraces the living and dead. We have nothing to fear, for God governs all things — including "ghosts" — with wisdom and love.

---

[18] Ibid.

[19] Ibid.

·· 22 ··

What is a plenary indulgence?

Dear Father Kerper,
When Pope Francis announced the Jubilee Year of Mercy, I suddenly started to hear a lot about indulgences. I thought such things had been abolished years ago. Isn't this superstition a mechanical type of spirituality? And is it true that indulgences can be passed on to dead people? Please explain.

Let's begin with the word "indulgence," the English form of the Latin word *indulgentia*. The Latin word can mean an act of kindness, tenderness, forbearance, and even the expression of fondness for another person. In "Church Latin," it primarily means putting aside a just punishment caused by sinful acts. Indulgences, when properly understood, simply reflect the mercy of God, who constantly bestows indulgences on human beings. During the Year of Mercy, Pope Francis linked special indulgences to specific things and acts, such as visiting a Holy Door, practicing works of mercy, and so forth.

Now, to get to a proper understanding of indulgences, we must grasp the relationship between forgiveness and punishment.

God, of course, graciously forgives all sins, even the worst. We experience this divine mercy preeminently in the sacrament of Penance, which firmly assures us that our sins are truly gone.

However, forgiveness does not necessarily free us from punishment. Some, of course, will quickly object: Where's the mercy? Why does God want to punish sin? Isn't this a contradiction?

From the merely human standpoint, we think of punishment as "settling scores." We punish wrongdoers by restricting their freedom, requiring some unpleasant work, or even causing pain or death. Such punishments are motivated primarily by the desire to restore justice—or to avenge misdeeds and deter other crimes.

By contrast, God's punishments always emerge from his merciful love. As such, God's penalties act as "medicine" to heal the self-inflicted wounds caused by personal sins, specifically the destruction of our friendship with God.

While these mysterious healing acts originate in God, they also involve Mary and all the saints. God draws them into his "healing project" through their union with the Body of Christ, which includes all baptized people, living and dead. This organic unity allows the goodness of each saint to benefit others. To put it another way, the "holy excess" of some saints gets transferred to people whose sins have made them "deficient," specifically by pulling them away from God and toward inferior goods or evil. God's punishment somehow corrects the sinner's disastrous turning away from God.

Here's an example. Imagine, say, a high school freshman who wants to become an engineer. He definitely needs to learn calculus. While in ninth grade he takes advanced algebra, plays video games during class, never pays attention, and fails the course. If he wants to learn calculus and have any hope of becoming an engineer, he must retake algebra during summer. In one sense, summer school

What is a plenary indulgence?

is a painful punishment for playing video games in class. But it also eventually "heals" the student's mind, which had become wounded by self-imposed ignorance of algebra.

At first glance, summer school appears to be a cruel punishment; but it's really an act of mercy because it restores to the student the possibility of reaching the goal of an engineering degree. Divine punishment does the same thing: it heals and returns the sinner to heaven's road. God's healing, as mentioned earlier, involves the "transfer" of spiritual goods within the Body of Christ, the communion of saints. How so? Theologians have offered various explanations, but perhaps the well-known story of Saint Augustine (354–430) and Saint Monica works best.

In his youth, Saint Augustine lived wildly, fathered an illegitimate son, and fell in with some brilliant people who vehemently rejected Christian faith. By any measure, Saint Augustine suffered from a massive deficiency of holiness. Saint Monica, his mother, clearly had "excess holiness," manifested by her infinite patience with her son, her constant prayer, and her resilient faith. Whereas Saint Augustine prayed little and behaved badly, Saint Monica's fervent prayer and goodness tipped the scales toward her son and fostered his spiritual healing and eventual conversion. Saint Monica, then, truly—and willingly—transferred her "spiritual goods" to her son. What happened to Saint Monica and Saint Augustine can happen to anyone. The same principle applies.

Now let's move into the "technical" area of indulgences. As early as the third century, the Church allowed sinners to seek the intercessory prayers of people on the verge of being martyred. Sinners believed that their prayerful association with heroic martyrs could remove or at least reduce the just punishments for their sins. Christians highly valued these prayers because they came from men and women who had given their lives and had surely gone to Heaven! The "holy excess" of martyrs was indisputable and freely transferable.

By the twelfth century, indulgences had become more common and increasingly regulated. Sad to say, these practices became widely misunderstood, distorted, and subject to abuse, especially by linking them with monetary exchange.

In 1967, Pope Blessed Paul VI strongly reaffirmed the Church's ancient teaching about indulgences, which flows from the doctrine of the communion of saints. Moreover, the Holy Father greatly simplified the system, dividing indulgences into two types: plenary and partial.

Plenary comes from the Latin word *plena*, which means "full." A plenary indulgence, then, frees a person from all punishment due to sin. In medical terms, it would be akin to a total healing of cancer, with the reversal of all the disease's consequences. In spiritual terms, a person granted a plenary indulgence would immediately enter into God's presence after dying, with all the wounds of sin healed. As an example, think of the Good Thief. Jesus said to him, "Truly, I say to you, today you will be with me in Paradise" (Luke 23:43).

A partial indulgence frees a person from some punishment due to sin. In the old system, which Paul VI modified, prayers and deeds were carefully calibrated according to difficulty, length, antiquity, and so forth. This excessive complexity, which emerged in the Middle Ages, sometimes promoted "spiritual accounting," which was not really traditional. The reformed system has restored pure, sincere, and simple prayer to its proper place.

As to the Year of Mercy, Pope Francis formally attached a plenary indulgence to the act of visiting a Holy Door. This is not superstition. Rather, the Holy Father affirmed this old tradition for two reasons: first, it provides a tangible focal point—a holy

What is a plenary indulgence?

location—for prayer and the experience of personal conversion; and second, it highlights how every baptized Catholic can act as an agent of divine mercy by praying for others, including the dead.

Indulgences, when understood in an authentic and balanced manner, should inflame our hearts with an even greater love for the Divine Mercy, whose mysterious ways eagerly draw people into His eternal embrace.

·· 23 ··
Can every sin, even abortion, be forgiven?

Dear Father Kerper,
A while ago I heard that Pope Francis had given all priests the power to forgive the sin of abortion. I'm confused. I was taught that every sin could be forgiven in Confession. Was I wrong? And why is abortion treated as a special case?

In September 2016, Pope Francis issued a letter proclaiming the Extraordinary Year of Mercy, which extended from December 8, 2015, to November 20, 2016. At the same time, he granted to all priests the power to forgive the sin of abortion. Like you, many other Catholics found this confusing. So let's sort out three distinct matters: first, the unlimited power of forgiveness through the sacrament of Penance; second, the purpose of penalties that the Church can impose on people who commit grave sins; and third, the Holy Father's passionate desire to proclaim God's mercy to all people.

All sins can be forgiven in the confessional

First, you are perfectly correct: all sins, even the worst, can be forgiven by any priest who hears a person's confession and grants sacramental absolution. Here, the Church simply imitates the forgiveness of Christ, who once said, "Therefore I tell you, every sin and blasphemy will be forgiven" (Matt. 12:31). The Lord excludes no sinner from forgiveness, except those who adamantly refuse forgiveness, the so-called blasphemy against the Holy Spirit, also known as final impenitence.

For many years, almost every priest in the world has had the power to forgive the sin of abortion if the person urgently desired absolution, expressed true sorrow, promised not to sin again, and wanted to be reconciled to God and the Church. Likewise, priests can forgive other grave sins such as murder, perjury, devil worship, and so on. No limits apply.

Forgiveness and Church penalties

Now, let's look at a second biblical text about Confession and forgiveness. On Easter night, the risen Christ appeared to the apostles, minus Thomas. Saint John wrote: "He breathed on them, and said to them, 'Receive the Holy Spirit. If you forgive the sins of any, they are forgiven; if you retain the sins of any, they are retained'" (John 20:22-23). This passage touches upon a key source of confusion: the distinction between forgiveness and being released from Church penalties. Priests have the capacity to forgive the sin of abortion, but only bishops have the capacity to release individuals from certain Church penalties.

For centuries, the Church has had a wide range of disciplinary tools to promote order and accountability, especially with regard to bishops, priests, consecrated religious, theologians, and people who work for Church institutions. These tools include excommunication, interdict, suspension, removal from office, and censure. Unlike some penalties imposed by civil authorities, Church sanctions never cause bodily harm, imprisonment, or loss of money, except if someone loses employment.

Excommunication and abortion

These carefully calibrated penalties identify specific sinful acts as more or less grave, relative to others. Hence, a very serious sin receives a very severe punishment: excommunication.

Canon 1398 states: "A person who procures a completed abortion incurs an automatic (*laete sententiae*) excommunication." Please note that this law also applies to everyone directly involved in the abortion: the ones who perform the abortion, those who pay for it, and anyone who compels a woman to abort her child.

Strange as it may seem, canon law does not impose an automatic excommunication on those who commit or assist in homicide. Why? Because abortion is always directed against a completely innocent and defenseless human being. By imposing an automatic excommunication, the Church wraps a mantle of maternal protection around unborn children who today have no legal protections in most Western societies.

The tricky word here is "automatic." The excommunication occurs only if the person knows about it. Since many women have no idea that they face excommunication, and many today may not even know that they are killing their children, the excommunication never happens.

As to those who knew about the excommunication and actually incurred it, the Holy Father's initiative allows all priests to reconcile them to the Church. Of course, in the United States, almost every priest has enjoyed this privilege for many years.

What is the Pope's point?

So, what's new here? Why did the Holy Father bother "legalizing" a practice already in wide use? First, his move drew vast media attention to the Church's desire to extend God's mercy to everyone through the sacrament of Penance. After all, many people, even well-instructed Catholics, were surprised that abortion could be forgiven. Second, the Holy Father's words about abortion were deeply pastoral, not legalistic. He wrote as a compassionate father, not an icy prosecutor. Here's what he said:

> I think in particular of all the women who have resorted to abortion. I am well aware of the pressure that has led them to this decision. I know that it is an existential and moral ordeal. I have met so many women who bear in their heart the scar of this agonizing and painful decision. What has happened is profoundly unjust; yet only understanding the truth of it can enable one not to lose hope. The forgiveness of God cannot be denied to one who has repented, especially when that person approaches the Sacrament of Confession with a sincere heart in order to obtain reconciliation with the Father.[20]

The Holy Father's beautiful words strike a perfect balance between mercy and justice; concern for women caught in the snare

---

[20] *Letter of His Holiness Pope Francis According to Which an Indulgence Is Granted to the Faithful on the Occasion of the Extraordinary Jubilee of Mercy*, September 1, 2015.

of abortion and their precious unborn children; terrible sin and the greater power of God's grace and forgiveness. Yes, perhaps the Holy Father's unexpected decision in September 2015 did cause some confusion, but it also offered a profound teaching moment and became an occasion to hear sincere words of mercy and to witness a powerful gesture of compassionate forgiveness.

PART IV

Our Peculiar Ecumenical Family: Our Faith and the Odd Traditions

·· 24 ··

Why are the psalms so violent?

> Dear Father Kerper,
> A few months ago I felt called to expand my prayer life beyond going to Mass. A friend urged me to begin praying the Liturgy of the Hours. I did so but was put off by all the psalms, which seem so violent, harsh, and angry. I don't understand why this is even called "Christian Prayer." Most of it comes from the Old Testament. And I want something that connects me personally with God. Can you suggest a better alternative?

You certainly deserve praise for trying to deepen your prayer life. Although the Liturgy of the Hours has disappointed you, I suggest you give it a second look.

Your comments about the psalms are understandable and on target. Indeed, many of these prayers—actually hymns meant for singing—are very strange and deeply troubling. Yet, from earliest times, the Church has embraced these prayers as her own.

Why did the Church settle on the psalms as the core of formal Christian prayer?

First, and most important, Jesus used the prayers Himself. As a devout Jewish man of His time, Jesus would have sung and recited the psalms from His early childhood and throughout His life. Even as He suffered on the Cross, He prayed Psalm 22, which begins, "My God, my God, why have you forsaken me?"

Because genuine Christian prayer is never solitary, but always in complete union with Christ, the psalms pass from the lips and tongue of Jesus on to the lips and tongues of Christians. To put it another way, we have in our mouths the same prayers that flowed from His mouth. We all speak together; no other prayers are like that. While the New Testament contains some inspired prayers, such as the beautiful canticles in Saint Paul's writings, Jesus never actually prayed them Himself.

Second, we use the psalms so much because they pull us away from ourselves and compel us to embrace the whole experience of humanity, which Jesus entered, endured, and redeemed.

This helps us to understand the harshness, anger, and gloominess of some psalms. These ancient prayers express the whole range of human emotions: joy and sorrow, confidence and fear, gratitude and disappointment, and so on. At a particular moment, we may be experiencing the opposite emotion: the psalms, however, foster solidarity with Christ and the whole of humanity, which concerns Him so intensely. When we pray the psalms as the "Voice of Christ," they finally begin to make sense.

Now, let's turn to the "un-Christian" passages in the psalms. One needn't go too far into the psalms before some very harsh words appear. Yes, some psalms pulsate with hatred, anger, and vengeance. How can these be the sentiments of Christ, who promoted peace, forgiveness, and reconciliation?

Here we need to distinguish between two levels of meaning: the literal and the spiritual.

Why are the psalms so violent?

Please remember that all the psalms originated in some specific historical situation, such as war, disaster, or serious personal sin. The literal psalm, then, is profoundly human in its heated emotions of anger and outright hatred.

Christians, however, "spiritualize" these psalms, directing the anger and hatred against the Evil One, not against other people. These psalms, then, remind us of the endless conflict between God's goodness and the Evil One, who offers constant resistance. All the psalms, even those that wail in lamentation over defeat and disaster, point us to the ultimate triumph of God's way. After all, they flow from the mouth of the risen—not defeated—Christ who prays with and for those still on their earthly journey.

As to your last point about seeking a "personal connection," the psalms help us to understand that we become connected with God through our membership in the Body of Christ, not as isolated individuals. Today, much popular spirituality misses this key point. Christian prayer is not primarily about "God and me" but "God and us." The plural, not the singular, takes precedence. Saint Augustine understood this so well. In his *Confessions* he wrote: "How loudly I cried out to you, my God, as I read the psalms of David, songs full of faith, outbursts of devotion with no room in them for the breath of pride!"

For Saint Augustine, the psalms cured him of his own excessive egoism by fusing his lips with those of Christ and the whole Church. Today, the psalms can do the same for any sincere Christian who approaches them with openness and just a little understanding. Lent, being a time of prayer, is a good time to try them again.

·· 25 ··

Was Christ born on Christmas? And what does Santa have to do with it?

Dear Father Kerper,
Someone told me that December 25 is definitely not the birthday of Jesus Christ. Was Christ born on Christmas or not? If not, why has the Church always claimed that Jesus was born on December 25? And how could people get so mixed up about something so important?

Before answering your question, we need to consider our contemporary understanding of birthdays and how it differs from that of the early Church. In our culture, we heavily emphasize "marking" the precise anniversary of everyone's birthdate. By doing this we remember and rejoice over the entire life of the person, not just his or her actual birth. For example, when we celebrate the birthday of Washington, Lincoln, or some other heroic person, we ponder his whole life, not just his or her actual birth.

Early Christians had a very different approach. Indeed, they did not like birthdays at all because such festivals were intertwined with the "old religions," which dabbled in astrology and the occult.

To distance themselves from old pagan practices, early Christians tended to celebrate the day of a person's death as his or her true birthday. This reflected the Christian belief that a person's physical birth mattered very little unless it culminated in eternal life, which begins at death. A holy death—not mere birth—deserves great celebration.

In keeping with this approach, Christians began to link the feasts of saints with the anniversaries of their deaths, never with their birthday, except for Mary, the Mother of the Lord (September 8) and Saint John the Baptist (June 24).

This brings us to your question: Is December 25 the real birthday of Christ? Yes, if you mean the day on which Christians have celebrated the Lord's birth almost universally from the earliest times. However, the Church has never definitively taught that Jesus was born on December 25; there is no conclusive documentary evidence, and Sacred Scripture mentions no date whatsoever.

This lack of evidence should not surprise us in the least. While we place great value on keeping precise records of births, deaths, and marriages, ancient people did not, especially among common people such as Jesus, Mary, and Joseph. Most people in Palestine probably had no idea of their exact birthdates, and illiterate parents had no way of keeping track of their children's birthdays. While they may have remembered the season of the child's birth, they probably forgot the day and even the year.

As to Christ, we must always remember that the Gospels were "written in reverse"—they begin with the final events of Christ's life: His Passion, death, and Resurrection. The familiar Christmas texts of Saint Matthew and Saint Luke were all written after the Passion accounts. Moreover, if these Christmas stories, which we love so much, had never been written or had been lost, nothing of our faith in Christ would change. After all, the Gospels of Saint

Was Christ born on Christmas?

Mark and Saint John say nothing at all about the birth of Jesus. For sure, the Christmas texts deepen our understanding of Christ and provide wonderful color to the story, but they are not essential. Hence, we do not really need to know the date of Christ's birth.

Now, let us turn to long-established belief that December 25 is indeed the birthday of Christ. The choice of this date was no mere accident or whim. It has a strong theological basis.

By about AD 360 (or even earlier), Roman Christians had begun to celebrate the birth of Christ on December 25. However, Christians in other regions had fixed his birthday on January 6 (in conjunction with the Epiphany). Others had it on April 20 and May 15. Gradually, however, December 25 became almost universal. If Jesus has no birth certificate, why pick December 25? Because of its proximity to the winter solstice, nature's turning point between light and darkness.

Some ancient theologians believed that the events of Christ's life were mysteriously synchronized with the movements of nature. The following text from Saint Augustine is a good example of such thought:

> Let us rejoice, my brothers! A happy day it is for us as well as for the nations of the world!
>
> This particular day [December 25] has been made special not by the sun we see but by its Creator, whom we can't see. When did this happen? When a Virgin Mother poured forth from her fertility, without the aid of her genitalia, Him whom we could see. All that was made possible by her Creator, whom we can't see.[21]

---

[21] Augustine of Hippo, *Sermo* CLXXXVI, *Sermons to the People*, trans. William Griffin (New York: Image Books, 2002), 66.

Later, Saint Augustine says:

> It's as good a day as any. The Winter Solstice. Fall changing into winter. The shortest day. With each succeeding day, the light becomes longer—Couldn't this signify the work of Christ?[22]

Saint Augustine and other Doctors of the Church derived the exact birthday of Jesus through classical theological reflection, not through Sacred Scripture. While the speculations of holy theologians such as Saint Augustine are certainly worthy of belief, they are not definitive.

Finally, there is another reason for December 25: The "old" Roman religion also proposed a relationship between nature and its own gods. Hence, Romans celebrated a feast called Natalis Solis Invincti, which rejoiced over the "rebirth" of the sun at the winter solstice. Many scholars have asserted that Christians simply baptized this old pagan festival, replacing the sun with the Son of God.

In terms of worship and prayer, Christmas Day—December 25—is the only universal focal point of Christians as they rejoice in the birth of Christ, the One who would suffer, die, and rise again. By celebrating the Lord's birthday on December 25, we unite ourselves with hundreds of believing generations spread over many centuries. Surely, the Lord must now regard December 25 as His only true birthday, for on that day alone millions say, "Happy Birthday!"

The True Story of Saint Nicholas

Many people learn fairy tales and Bible stories simultaneously during early childhood. As a result, when the fairy tales dissolve as a

---

[22] Ibid., 71.

Was Christ born on Christmas?

child matures, the stories about Jesus can also lose their credibility. Amid this jumble of childhood stories, one must distinguish between fanciful fabrications and truths rooted in history.

Let's begin with Santa Claus. We know for certain that a man named Nicholas was born in Asia Minor (modern-day Turkey), served as bishop of Myra, died around 350, and soon became honored as a great saint. Although we lack precise historical documentation, it's highly probable that he assisted the poor, healed the sick, and interceded with God for people in need. Over time, stories about the kindness and generosity of Nicholas spread throughout Europe and other parts of the world.

Gradually, Nicholas of Myra evolved into the figure now known as Santa Claus, a name derived from the Latin word *sancta* (saint) and the last part of the name Nicholas. Strictly speaking, then, Santa Claus/Saint Nicholas did indeed exist. He is not at all like the tooth fairy and the Easter Bunny.

In a sense, Santa Claus/Saint Nicholas acts in the world today whenever people imitate, even unconsciously, his goodness and generosity by giving gifts to others, especially children. After all, every loving deed somehow originates in God, who is love, and when someone like Saint Nicholas inspires gift giving, we can say that he somehow truly shares in the act.

Now we come to the Christmas story, which you learned as a child alongside the Santa Claus story. At first glance it seems to be the same thing: a story with a genuine historical root but overlaid with untrue and fanciful details. But the Christmas story, at least the parts recounted in Sacred Scripture, differs fundamentally from fairy tales such as the full-blown Santa story.

First, Christmas commemorates a true historical fact: the birth of Jesus of Nazareth, the one acclaimed by many as Messiah and Son of God. Today, there's no serious historian—whether believer or unbeliever—who would challenge His existence. The documentation, although sparse, is persuasive.

In addition to reporting the birth of Jesus, the Gospel writers included many secondary details, such as the star of Bethlehem, shepherds, magi, angels, and so forth. These well-known elements go far beyond "raw history" by asserting truths of faith about Jesus, such as His true familial link with King David, His life and death as ultimate fulfillment of Israelite prophecy, and His mission to the Gentiles.

These elements of the biblical Christmas story differ from the fanciful stories about Santa Claus. Consider the famous poem "The Night before Christmas," written by Clement Clarke Moore in 1822. Moore wrote his poem to entertain and delight young children. His charming description of Santa's nocturnal visits on Christmas Eve is entirely fictional and unrelated to the historical Saint Nicholas. By contrast, the biblical Christmas story is not entertainment for children, but an essential part of Sacred Scripture that expresses basic truths about Christ's origin and identity.

I hasten to add that much traditional imagery associated with the Christmas story goes far beyond what the Gospels state. Figures in nativity scenes such as the little drummer boy, talking mice, and the kneeling Santa are all innovations, not part of the biblical account. Although cute, they can confuse children by mixing the fanciful with the biblical.

As the Christmas season approaches I hope this explanation will help you to rediscover the essential truth we celebrate: that God, who is love, sent His Son to us, and that everyone who is joined to Him—including Santa Claus/Saint Nicholas, your parents, and you—can extend divine love into the world.

·· 26 ··

Why do priests get moved? Why do deacons do so much of the priestly work now?

Dear Father Kerper,
Recently our pastor was moved to another parish after spending many years with us. Everyone loved him, and we felt as if we knew him very well. I don't understand why priests have to move around so much. This seems to harm parishes by causing uncertainty and too much change. A Protestant friend told me that her parish picks its own pastor and decides how long the pastor stays with them. This seems like a better system. At least people get to decide.

Thank you for your question. I commend you for posing this question during this difficult transition. Eventually every Catholic has an experience like yours: a beloved and respected priest suddenly moves on and gets replaced by a stranger. For a time, everything in the parish seems unsettled as people try to adjust to the new pastor's personality and leadership style. Quite naturally people will feel grief, fear, and even anger. Yet we must always recognize that the changing of pastors, although painful, is rooted in the very structure of Holy Orders, the sacrament that "produces" bishops, priests, and deacons.

Notice that the Church uses the term "Holy Orders." When the bishop ordains a man to the priesthood, the man is never ordained for a single community, but for service within the Order of Presbyters, also called the presbyterate. (By the way, *presbyter* is the Greek word for "elder." The English word "priest" comes from *presbyter*.)

In every diocese the whole presbyterate serves the whole body of the baptized faithful, grouped into parishes. Although parishioners tend to regard their pastor as belonging exclusively to them, the pastor actually "belongs" to the diocese, not to the parish. Moreover, the priest never acts independently of the bishop and other priests. The *Catechism of the Catholic Church* puts it this way: "Priests exercise their ministry from within the presbyterium of the diocese, under the direction of their bishop" (no. 877). In other words, the pastor always operates as a member of a priestly team, never alone.

This leads to your point about the common practice of Protestant congregations' recruiting, hiring, and dismissing their own pastors. This approach, which surely has some appeal, reveals a fundamental difference between the Catholic and many Protestants' understandings of the Church, notably the relationship between the universal Church and the local congregation.

From the Catholic perspective, we belong originally and primarily to the universal Church and only secondarily to the parish. In the standard Protestant view, a person belongs primarily to the local church. As such, many Protestant congregations, but surely not all, "call" and even ordain their own pastors. By contrast, Catholic

Why do priests get moved?

pastors are never called by parishes; instead they are sent by the bishop.

Our practice necessarily follows from the Catholic understanding that the whole Church provides ministry to all Catholics through Holy Orders, which generates members for three collective orders: the episcopacy (bishops), the presbyterate (priests), and the diaconate (deacons).

This, of course, has its roots in the Lord's decision to form and send forth a group called the Twelve Apostles. The *Catechism of the Catholic Church* states, "Chosen together, they were also sent out together, and their fraternal unity would be the service of the fraternal communion of all the faithful" (no. 877). No local Catholic community ever generates its own pastors. They always come from the broader Church.

So far, I've given a theological explanation. So now, let's consider the practical reasons for changing pastors.

First, priests, like all human beings, have a great variety of personalities, backgrounds, talents, and deficiencies. As such, no single priest, no matter how good and dedicated, can meet all the pastoral needs of a specific parish, which itself undergoes constant change. For example, at some point in its life a parish may need a strong administrator rather than an inspiring preacher. At another time, a parish may need a priest more comfortable with young people than in a hospital setting. As the parish changes over time, sometimes drastically, it may need an entirely different kind of pastor.

Second, the regular rotation of pastors makes possible the emergence of new lay leadership. Because human beings generally avoid change, parishioners can easily fall into ruts, allowing small intertwined groups—really cliques—to occupy all positions of service and authority, thereby blocking out new people. Usually people don't intend for this to happen, but it often does. This, unfortunately, can paralyze a parish.

While some peculiar circumstances may justify—and even require—the unusual longevity of a particular pastor, most parishes benefit immensely by regularly changing their pastors.

I encourage you to keep an open mind about your new pastor. Pray for him and your fellow parishioners so that everyone can move forward together, trusting that our Catholic practice of rotating pastors somehow reflects the wisdom of the Lord, who Himself gave shape to the essential structures of the Church.

What is a lay deacon, and what can he do?

In recent years, the Catholic bishops of the United States have ordained more than fifteen thousand men to the permanent diaconate. About twenty-five serve in the Diocese of Manchester, New Hampshire.

Although permanent deacons seem new, the order of deacons is one of the Church's oldest institutions.

Notice that I use the term "order of deacons." The word "order" means that a particular group within the church has a sacred origin and is an essential part of the Church's permanent structure. Men become deacons through ordination—"being ordered"—by the bishop. As such, all deacons are members of the clergy, along with bishops and priests. There is no such thing as a "lay deacon."

In Acts 6:1-6, Saint Luke describes how the Apostles themselves established the diaconate, a term derived from the Greek word *diakonos*, meaning domestic service. In fact, waiting on tables was the original task of deacons. As the church developed, deacons became the official dispensers of charity. We see this most clearly in the story of Saint Lawrence, the Roman deacon who outraged the emperor by giving the goods of the Church to the poor, rather than to the state.

While service has always been the deacon's primary ministry, tradition indicates that deacons were also ministers of word and sacrament. For example, Saint Stephen, deacon and first martyr, preached publicly. And tradition shows that deacons distributed the Precious Blood at Mass. Today, deacons can also baptize, serve as the Church's official witness at weddings, and offer blessings.

Deacons appear to be "new" because for many centuries the priesthood embodied all forms of official ministry. The distinctiveness and diversity of the triple form of ordained ministry—bishop, priest, and deacon—became virtually invisible. Then the Second Vatican Council restored the diaconate as a permanent order, thereby recovering the diversity of ordained ministries present at the Church's origins. As such, deacons are not "half priests" or "vested laity" who fill ministerial gaps. Rather, the visible presence of deacons in parish life shows forth the variety of distinctive ordained ministries working together in the Body of Christ.

Many dioceses, such as my own Diocese of Manchester, have begun a process to expand the order of deacons within their borders.

Who is a permanent deacon and what does he do?

By virtue of his or her baptism, each and every member of the Catholic Church enjoys new life in Christ, a sharing in His divine life. In light of this participation, all the baptized share in Christ's mission and priesthood—to sanctify, to teach, to guide, each according to the gifts each has received. Thus, all members of the

Catholic Church are called to share their gifts as Christ did, to minister to others in the name of Jesus.

God calls some men through the Church to share in Christ's priesthood through the sacrament of Orders. They are configured to Christ. The bishop shares fully in the ministerial priesthood of Christ, while priests and deacons share in the one, same priesthood.

Thus, the deacon is an ordained minister of the Church, a member of the clergy. The deacon works collaboratively with bishops, priests, and existing staff members of a parish or institution. They work together to build up the Body of Christ.

Since all ordained ministers in the Church are called to serve through word, sacrament, and charity, bishops, priests, and deacons exercise these services in various ways. As a minister of word, a deacon proclaims the Gospel, preaches, and teaches in the name of the Church. As a minister of sacrament, a deacon baptizes, leads the faithful in prayer, witnesses marriages, and conducts wake and funeral services. As a minister of charity, a deacon is a leader in identifying the needs of others and in calling God's people into service to meet these needs.

As mentioned earlier, the title "deacon" comes from the Greek word *diakonos*, which means "servant." The deacon is an "icon," or sacramental sign of Christ, who came "not to be served but to serve" (Mark 10:45). Once ordained by the bishop, the deacon enters into a new set of relationships: he is permanently and publicly configured to Christ the Servant; he shares in the overall responsibility of the bishop to care for the people in the diocese, and he becomes an integral part of the clergy of the diocese, assisting the bishop and the priests in serving the needs of the diocese.

No matter what specific services a deacon performs, they all flow from his sacramental identity. In other words, it is not only what a deacon does, but who a deacon is, that is important.

Becoming a deacon involves a vocation from God; it is not simply a volunteer job or ministry. Therefore, a person becomes a deacon not out of personal desire or interest, but for the common good of the Church as determined by the bishop. It is for these reasons that the selection, discernment, and formation of deacon candidates are rigorous and intense efforts. The entire formation process, in fact, is a journey of discernment. Through systematic opportunities for prayer, spiritual direction, formal coursework, and pastoral-skills development, the candidate is able to reflect critically on his life and the various vocations to which he might be called. This process of discernment continues to the moment of ordination.

Ordination bestows a permanent character on a person. Once ordained, the deacon is always a deacon, regardless of where he is or what he is doing, just as a priest or a bishop is always a priest or bishop, regardless of where he is or what he is doing. Ministry in the church is not something that happens only within a church building, during a church-sponsored activity, or at liturgy. A deacon is just as engaged in his ministry when he is at work or engaged in other activities not directly related to the Church. It is precisely in his leadership and presence outside formal Church structures that the deacon can often enable and empower others to exercise their own diaconal responsibilities as Christians.

Ministry is a tapestry. We need all the threads to appreciate the richness and diversity of the whole, and each of these threads leads us to Christ. We want to be a diocese that encourages all ministry, lay and ordained, for the building up of the Body of Christ. The deacon, as an ordained minister, has a permanent and a public responsibility for a ministry of word, sacrament, and charity. Through ordination, he becomes an icon of Christ the Servant. When a person sees the deacon, the person should see and experience Christ in service to the world.

·· 27 ··

Are Guardian Angels real?

Dear Father Kerper,
A friend of mine, who is a very devout Catholic, always talks about her so-called Guardian Angel. I heard about these angels when I was a child. Now that I'm an adult I regard them as legends or myths made up to make children feel safe. Are Guardian Angels real? Is there anything in the Bible about them?

As we grow into adulthood and become more sophisticated, we tend to dismiss some religious beliefs we learned as children. Guardian Angels fall into this category of "childish beliefs" that seem nice but also far-fetched. Rather than tossing them out completely, I suggest that you consider a deeper and more mature interpretation of what Guardian Angels really are.

Let's begin with their existence. The *Catechism of the Catholic Church* clearly affirms their reality. It repeats the words of Saint Basil the Great: "Beside each believer stands an angel protector and shepherd leading him to life" (no. 336). The *Catechism* uses this brief text to show that belief in Guardian Angels is both ancient (Saint Basil lived in the fourth century) and espoused by a highly reputable and holy theologian (Saint Basil is called "the Great" precisely because his works are considered of the highest quality).

More important, of course, is the biblical background. According to the Gospel of Matthew, Jesus once gathered children to Himself and said, "Take care that you do not despise one of these little ones; for, I tell you, in heaven their angels continually see the face of my Father in heaven" (Matt. 18:10-11). In the Old Testament, the book of Tobit has a scene in which Tobit spoke of the "guardian angel" of his son Tobias. The old man said: "For a good angel will accompany him; his journey will be successful, and he will come back in good health" (Tob. 5:22).

While the Catholic theological tradition, especially in the Middle Ages, has extensive speculation about angels, the Church's official teaching is remarkably reserved. It affirms just two succinct points: first, God's creation includes a multitude of noncorporeal personal beings; and second, these beings somehow share in the beneficent works of God.

Drawing upon these two points, we see that Catholic belief in Guardian Angels is not exclusively—or even primarily—about angels. Rather, the teaching beautifully expresses our Catholic understanding of the human person and the way God generally acts in the created cosmos. We learn three things here.

First, belief in Guardian Angels strongly reaffirms the Catholic belief in the infinite value of the individual human person. In a world of anonymity and depersonalized service, God refuses to offer "generic" care from the anonymous angelic ranks. Rather, God provides each human person with specialized care from one specific being. By doing this, God tenderly affirms that every person is unrepeatable, unique, and deserving of individual and personal attention.

Second, Guardian Angels reflect God's "style" of dealing with created reality. Rather than acting unilaterally, God forever invites and enables other beings—human and angelic—to share in God's own vast work. God, of course, needs no help. But God's intense desire to share the divine life with created beings leads God to create and enlist others in guiding creation to fulfill its proper end.

Third, the mystery of the Guardian Angels reminds us that creation is essentially good and that the general direction of the universe is toward the fulfillment—not the frustration—of God's plan. Unseen by the human eye, goodness in the form of invisible angelic beings abounds everywhere, advancing God's design in ways we can scarcely imagine.

Saint Bernard, whose words are quoted in the Office of Readings for the memorial of the Guardian Angels, said this of the Guardian Angels: "Brothers, let us love God's angels with sincere affection: they will be our co-heirs at some future time.... They cannot be vanquished, nor led astray, still less can they lead us astray.... They are faithful, they are wise, they are powerful; what have we to fear?"

Your childhood belief in Guardian Angels probably gave you a sense of safety. Now, as an adult, this same belief should fill you with wonder about God's creation, appreciation for your own role as a coworker with God, and joyful hope that the vast goodness of God will ultimately prevail.

About the Author
Father Michael Kerper

Father Michael Kerper grew up in Philadelphia, attended Catholic schools as a boy, and then studied politics and economics at LaSalle University, labor relations at the University of Massachusetts at Amherst, and moral theology at Mount St. Mary's Seminary in Emmitsburg, Maryland. Ordained in 1985 for the Diocese of Manchester, Father Kerper has worked as a parish priest throughout New Hampshire.

Sophia Institute

Sophia Institute is a nonprofit institution that seeks to nurture the spiritual, moral, and cultural life of souls and to spread the Gospel of Christ in conformity with the authentic teachings of the Roman Catholic Church.

Sophia Institute Press fulfills this mission by offering translations, reprints, and new publications that afford readers a rich source of the enduring wisdom of mankind.

Sophia Institute also operates two popular online Catholic resources: CrisisMagazine.com and CatholicExchange.com.

Crisis Magazine provides insightful cultural analysis that arms readers with the arguments necessary for navigating the ideological and theological minefields of the day. *Catholic Exchange* provides world news from a Catholic perspective as well as daily devotionals and articles that will help you to grow in holiness and live a life consistent with the teachings of the Church.

In 2013, Sophia Institute launched Sophia Institute for Teachers to renew and rebuild Catholic culture through service to Catholic education. With the goal of nurturing the spiritual, moral, and cultural life of souls, and an abiding respect for the role and work of teachers, we strive to provide materials and programs that are at once enlightening to the mind and ennobling to the heart; faithful and complete, as well as useful and practical.

Sophia Institute gratefully recognizes the Solidarity Association for preserving and encouraging the growth of our apostolate over the course of many years. Without their generous and timely support, this book would not be in your hands.

www.SophiaInstitute.com
www.CatholicExchange.com
www.CrisisMagazine.com
www.SophiaInstituteforTeachers.org

Sophia Institute Press® is a registered trademark of Sophia Institute.
Sophia Institute is a tax-exempt institution as defined by the Internal Revenue Code, Section 501(c)(3). Tax I.D. 22-2548708.

Printed by Libri Plureos GmbH in Hamburg, Germany